How to File Your Own Bankruptcy

(or How to Avoid it)

WITH FORMS

By Edward A. Haman
Attorney at Law

Admitted to practice in Florida, Hawaii and Michigan

Sphinx International, Inc.
1725 Clearwater-Largo Rd., S.
Post Office Box 2005
Clearwater, FL 34617
Phone 800-226-5291

Note: The law changes constantly and is subject to different interpretations. It is up to you to check it thoroughly before relying on it. Neither the author nor the publisher guarantees the outcome of the uses to which this material is put.

First Edition, December, 1990

ISBN 0-913825-32-8

Library of Congress Catalog Number: 90-63136

Manufactured in the United States of America.

This publication is designed to provide accurate and authoritative information in regard to the subject matter covered. It is sold with the understanding that the publisher is not engaged in rendering legal, accounting or other professional services. If legal advice or other expert assistance is required, the service of a competent professional person should be sought.

-From a Declaration of Principles jointly adopted by a Committee of the American Bar Association and a Committee of Publishers.

Published by Sphinx Publishing, a division of Sphinx International, Inc., Post Office Box 2005, Clearwater, Florida 34617-2005. This publication is available by mail for $19.95 (plus Florida sales tax if applicable) plus $1.50 for shipping.

TABLE OF CONTENTS

PART THREE: PREPARATION FOR BANKRUPTCY

PART FOUR: BANKRUPTCY PROCEDURE

INTRODUCTION TO SELF-HELP LAW BOOKS

Whenever you shop for a product or service you are faced with a variety of different levels of quality and price. In deciding upon which one to buy you make a cost/value analysis based upon your willingness to pay and the quality you desire.

When buying a car you decide whether you want transportation, comfort, status or sex appeal, and you decide among such choices as a Chevette, a Lincoln, a Rolls Royce or a Porche. Before making a decision you usually weigh the merits of each against the cost.

When you get a headache, you can take a pain reliever such as aspirin or you can go to a medical specialist for a neurological examination. Given this choice most people, of course, take a pain reliever, since it only costs pennies whereas a medical examination would cost hundreds of dollars and take a lot of time. This is usually a very logical choice because very rarely is anything more than a pain reliever needed for a headache. But in some cases a headache may indicate a brain tumor and failing to go to a specialist right away can result in complications. Should everyone with a headache go to a specialist? Of course not, but people treating their own illnesses must realize that they are taking a chance, based upon their cost/value analysis of the situation, that they are taking the most logical option.

The same cost/value analysis must be made in deciding to do one's own legal work. Many legal situations are very simple, requiring a simple form and no complicated analysis. Anyone with a little intelligence and a book of instructions can handle the matter simply.

But there is always the chance that there is a complication involved which only a lawyer would notice. To simplify the law into a book like this, often several legal cases must be condensed into a single sentence or paragraph. Otherwise, the book would be several hundred pages long and too complicated for most people. However, this simplification necessarily leaves out many details and nuances which would apply to special or unusual situations. Also, there are many ways to interpret most legal questions. Your case may come before a judge who disagrees with the analysis of our author.

Therefore, in deciding to use a self-help law book and to do your own legal work you must realize that you are making a cost/value analysis and deciding that the chance that your case will not turn out to your satisfaction is outweighed by the money you will save by doing it yourself. Most people doing their own simple legal matters will probably never have a problem. But occasionally someone may find out that it ended up costing them more to have an attorney straighten out the situation than it would have if they had hired an attorney to begin with.

Keep this in mind while handling your case and be sure to consult an attorney if you feel you might need further guidance.

INTRODUCTION

IS THIS BOOK FOR YOU? You are probably feeling burdened by your financial situation, or else you wouldn't be reading this. If you are like most Americans, you are probably struggling to make payments on a mortgage, car loan, various credit cards, and possibly a student loan, home improvement loan, or other consumer debts. This book is designed specifically for you. It will help you analyze your situation, decide whether you should file for bankruptcy, and guide you through the steps to either avoid bankruptcy or get through the bankruptcy procedure. This is not a law school course, but a practical guide to get you through "The System" as easily as possible.

This book presents fairly simplified procedures for use by non-attorneys, therefore, it does not contain all the possible "loopholes" or "tricks of the trade" which an experienced bankruptcy lawyer might use to gain a little extra advantage. On the other hand, for many people, these legal details either don't apply, or their advantage will be offset by not having to pay the fee of an experienced bankruptcy attorney.

If you are fairly to extremely wealthy, or have extensive and complicated investments, you will need a lawyer. However, this book will still help you to understand the system and work with your lawyer more effectively.

This book is not designed for corporate, partnership, or business-related bankruptcies. If your business is in financial trouble, you need to consult an attorney.

BE SURE TO READ THIS ENTIRE BOOK, ESPECIALLY SECTION 10 ON UNDERSTANDING LEGAL FORMS, BEFORE YOU BEGIN PREPARING ANY OF THE FORMS IN THIS BOOK. For any form in this book, you will need to make copies of the form. Save the originals in order to make more copies if you need them.

PART ONE: BASICS

SECTION 1. WHAT IS BANKRUPTCY?

Simply stated, bankruptcy is a legal procedure which allows you to get out of oppressive debt, and get a fresh start financially.

The concept of bankruptcy goes back at least to the time of the Old Testament of the Bible, where it states: "At the end of every seven years you shall grant a release and this is the manner of the release: every creditor shall release what he has lent to his neighbor..." -Deuteronomy 15:1-2.

In the United States, the importance of bankruptcy was recognized at the time of our nation's birth, and was made a part of the U.S. Constitution. Article I, Section 8 of the U.S. Constitution gives Congress the power to establish "uniform laws on the subject of bankruptcies throughout the United States." In 1800 Congress enacted the first bankruptcy laws.

Today there exists a comprehensive set of federal laws which govern bankruptcy. There are so many bankruptcies filed each year that there is a special division of the federal court system devoted exclusively to bankruptcy. So if you need to file for bankruptcy, you can be sure you will not be alone!

The bankruptcy procedure serves two purposes. First, it allows you to change your financial situation. Second, it gets your creditors off your back while you make this change.

You also have a choice about changing your situation. You can choose either of two procedures. The first is traditional bankruptcy, where your debts are forgiven altogether. The other procedure is referred to as a "re-organization," "wage-earner plan," or "payment plan." In this procedure, you arrange to pay off some or all of your debts according to a payment plan that you can handle on your income. Although this is technically not "bankruptcy," it is a part of the bankruptcy law and will be referred to in this book as a bankruptcy.

Traditional bankruptcy is covered in Chapter 7 of the federal Bankruptcy Act, and is often referred to as a "Chapter 7." The payment plan procedure is covered in Chapter 13 of the Bankruptcy Act, and is referred to as a "Chapter 13." These procedures will be discussed in greater detail in later Sections of this book. To help avoid confusion with "chapters" of the Bankruptcy Act, this book is divided into "Sections" instead of into "Chapters."

SECTION 2. THE LEGAL SYSTEM

This Section will give you a general introduction to the legal system of the bankruptcy court. Most people have a concept of the way the legal system SHOULD be, which usually does not match the realities of the system. If you don't learn to accept the realities, you will experience much stress and frustration.

Fortunately, bankruptcy is one area of the law that is a bit more "cut and dried" and predictable (in most cases) than many other areas.

A. RULES.

Our legal system is a system of rules. There are basically three types of rules:
1. Rules of Law: such as defining a "debt" and describing what property can be kept after bankruptcy.
2. Rules of Procedure: such as requiring court papers to be in a certain form, or filed within a certain time.
3. Rules of Evidence: these require facts to be proven in a certain way.

In bankruptcy it is not usually necessary to be concerned with rules of evidence, which automatically makes this an easier area of the law to deal with. In addition, the rules of law and procedure are so well defined that they are not nearly as complicated and subject to interpretation as in many other areas. For most middle-class Americans, bankruptcy is mostly filling out certain forms, filing them with the court, and attending a couple of meetings. As long as you provide the court with accurate and complete information about your finances, you shouldn't have any difficulties.

B. DON'T PANIC!

This is the basic rule of this book. If, as you read, you find yourself thinking "I'll never be able to do this myself," KEEP READING. By the end of the book you'll see that it is really a simple matter.

The advice "DON'T PANIC" also applies to dealing with the court. The United States is divided into numerous "districts," and each district has its own bankruptcy court. Each court has a court clerk, and may have some local rules. It is possible that the clerk in your district will tell you that one of your papers is not exactly correct in its form or content. This happens to lawyers with many years of experience, so there is no need to feel bad if it happens to you. If this happens to you, all you can do is relax, find out exactly what the clerk wants, and do it the clerk's way. Similar to the Army, there is the right way, the wrong way, and the clerk's way. Only the clerk's way will get you what you want.

C. THE SYSTEM.

Although bankruptcy is relatively simple and straight-forward, there are a few realities of our nation's legal system that can apply to all areas of the law to some degree. A brief mention of these realities may prepare you in the event you encounter any of them.

THE SYSTEM IS NOT PERFECT. The rules are designed to apply to all persons in all situations. This can sometimes lead to an unfair result. (An example relates to the federal "ERISA" law, which was designed to assure that certain retirement benefits are preserved. In applying a general legal principal, that the existence of complete federal laws prohibit states from making laws on the same subject, the U.S. Supreme Court ruled that states can't make laws which further protect these ERISA benefits.) It is also possible for a judge to make a bad call, or for someone to cheat and not get caught (such as by not telling the truth even under oath). As a well-known and respected judge once said to the young attorney: "This is court of law, young man, not a court of justice!"

JUDGES DON'T ALWAYS FOLLOW THE RULES. This is a shocking discovery for many young lawyers. After spending three years in law school learning legal theory, and after spending countless hours preparing for a hearing in which all of the law is on your side, you find that the judge isn't going to pay any attention to legal theories and the law. As one judge is known to have put it: "In my courtroom, the law is what I say it is." Many judges are going to make a decision simply on the judge's personal view of what seems fair under the circumstances (even if he doesn't take the time to fully understand the circumstances, and even if he has a strange idea of "fairness"). The judge will then find some way to try to justify his decision, even if it means distorting or ignoring the existing law.

THE SYSTEM IS SLOW. Even lawyers get frustrated at how long it can take to get a case completed (especially if they don't get paid until it is done). Things generally take longer than you would expect. Patience is required to get through the system with a minimum of stress. Don't get angry and let your frustration show.

NO TWO CASES ARE ALIKE. If your friends or co-workers learn that you've filed for bankruptcy, you can be sure you will be getting a lot of "legal" advice from them. DON'T LISTEN TO THEM. Everyone has their own experience to relate, or a story to tell about a friend or relative who has gone through bankruptcy. DON'T LISTEN TO THEM. They probably used an attorney, and attorneys are not always good about explaining the law and procedure to their clients. The attitude of many attorneys is: "I know what I'm doing, trust me, you don't need to know all of the legal details." After reading this book, you will know more about bankruptcy than any of your friends. Also, your case is not exactly the same as the one they will want to tell you about, so you can't expect your experience will be the same.

D. THE PLAYERS.

Law and the legal system are often compared to games, and just like games, it is important to understand who the players are.

1. THE JUDGE.

The judge has the power to determine whether your debts can be discharged (or whether your payment plan is accepted). In bankruptcy court, the judge is a U.S. District Court Judge, who is appointed to his position for life by the President. Bankruptcy judges have large caseloads, and like it best when your case can be conducted quickly and without hassles. This means that you want to be sure that your papers are completed correctly and with complete and accurate information. Most likely, you will only see the judge at your final hearing, which will only take a few minutes. The most important thing is to show respect for the judge. This means that you will answer the judge's questions as simply and to the point as possible. Under no circumstances will you get into an argument with the judge, or with a creditor while you are before the judge. You will always follow the judge's instructions without argument or complaint.

2. THE COURT CLERK.

The job of the clerk is to handle the filing of papers, the scheduling of hearings, and the maintaining of the court's files. Be sure you are friendly and cooperative toward the people in the clerk's office. If you make a clerk your enemy there is no end to the trouble he or she can cause you. Generally, the clerk has no interest in the outcome of your case, but is only interested that all of the paperwork is in order. The clerk has the power to accept or reject your papers. If the clerk wants something changed in your papers, just find out what he wants and do it. If you happen to encounter a particularly unfriendly clerk, try to understand that he frequently deals with frustrated, angry and rude people. You'll get much farther by showing him that you are happy to cooperate and are patient with the slowness of the system, than by being just another rude person causing him stress.

3. THE TRUSTEE.

After you file your first papers, your case will be assigned to a trustee. The trustee's job is to make sure that your papers are complete and accurate, assure that all of your creditors are notified about your bankruptcy, and generally assure that your case proceeds properly and is ready for final hearing with the judge. The trustee works for the court, and is a kind of middle-man between you, your creditors, and the court.

4. THE CREDITORS.

These are the people and companies that you owe money to. These people will not be happy about your bankruptcy, because it means they will probably not get paid. Some of them may get to take back the property they sold you, and some of them will get nothing. Some of them may be very hostile, and some of them will just accept your bankruptcy as part of the risk of doing business (after all, they encouraged you to buy on credit). Once you file for bankruptcy your creditors can no longer bother you for payment. You may stop making payments once you file, except on items you don't want to lose (such as your mortgage and car payments). All your creditor can do is either object to the court that you don't qualify for bankruptcy, or object to your plan for how their debt is to be handled. In most cases, neither objection meets with much success.

5. LAWYERS.

This either refers to your lawyer (which will be discussed more in Chapter 4 of this book), or to your creditor's lawyer. Generally, in bankruptcy proceedings there will be little difference between dealing with your creditor or his attorney. Many lawyers are dignified and polite in the dealings with "the other side" in a case. These lawyers will try to get the best deal for their client, and will do it in a polite and honest, but firm and business-like, manner. Other lawyers are truly nasty people, who are impolite and can't deal with their opponent in a civilized manner. They will not hesitate to make threats and lie about the law in an attempt to intimidate you. These lawyers simply can't be reasoned with, and you shouldn't try. If you encounter one of these lawyers, simply don't speak to him. Just address all of your statements to the trustee or the judge instead (very respectfully and politely of course). If you are uncertain of the law as stated by such an attorney, you may wish to consult an attorney yourself.

SECTION 3. BANKRUPTCY LAW AND PROCEDURE

This Section will give you an overview of the law and the procedure of bankruptcy. We will get into the details and the "how to" later, but first it is important to get a more general and overall view of the process.

A. IN GENERAL.

The idea of the bankruptcy law is to give you a fresh start, free from your previous debts, with enough assets to live on and get you started again. The law sets up different classes of debts and property, which determine what property you can keep, what property you can't keep, and whether and how much your creditors get paid.

SIX-YEAR LIMITATION, ETC. There are some limits as to how often you can use bankruptcy. You may not file under Chapter 7 if (1) you obtained a discharge under a Chapter 7, 11, 12 or 13 petition filed within the past six months, (2) you had a Chapter 7 case dismissed within the past 180 days because you violated a court order, or (3) you had a Chapter 7 case dismissed within the past 180 days because you asked for dismissal after a creditor asked for the automatic stay to be lifted. However, these limits do not apply to Chapter 13 cases, which may be filed at any time.

Each piece of property you own will be classified as either "exempt" (which means you may be able to keep it), or as "non-exempt" (which means you will have to turn it over to the trustee). Although the bankruptcy act is a Federal law, the available exemptions are different in each state. APPENDIX B of this book will tell you how to determine the property which is exempt in your state, and this will be discussed in more detail later. Most states will allow you to keep a certain dollar value of real estate, a car, tools used in your profession, insurance policies, clothing, household furnishings, retirement benefits, public benefits (such as workers' compensation and unemployment), and other personal items. These are "exempt" property. However, exempt property may still be lost if you borrowed money to buy it and don't keep up your payments.

This brings us to the classification of debts as either "secured" or "unsecured". A secured debt is one which is covered by a certain piece of property. The most common examples are home mortgages and car loans. The papers you signed when you borrowed the money specifically state that if you don't pay, the lender may take the property. You may not keep such property unless you pay for it, even if it would otherwise be exempt property in your state. So, if you don't want to lose your home or car, you will have to arrange a payment plan acceptable to your lender, or just keep your payments current.

An unsecured debt is not covered by any property. An example of an unsecured debt is a department store credit card or a VISA card. In these cases, the lender does not get paid and does not get any property either. Even if you bought your dining room furniture with your credit card, it is still an unsecured debt (unless you also signed some additional paper which states that the property secured the loan).

One other part of the law that is significant is that there are a few types of debts that cannot be discharged in bankruptcy. The four most common types are taxes you owe, government guaranteed student loans, child support, and alimony. So even if you go through a bankruptcy, you will still have to pay these debts.

The bankruptcy procedure is really quite simple, and can be viewed as a four-step process. First, you prepare and file your Petition and various supporting documents. This is simply a request for the court to discharge your debts according to the law, and information about your income, expenses, assets and debts.

Second, the trustee sends notices to all of your creditors to advise them that you have filed for bankruptcy. This gives them an opportunity to be sure you have given correct information in your petition, and to raise any questions or objections.

Third, you have a meeting with the trustee and your creditors (if they show up). This is when any questions or objections are discussed and settled.

Fourth, you attend a hearing, at which time the judge will discharge your debts. This may even be a mass-discharge of many cases at one time, in which you and many others obtain a discharge at the same time.

B. CHAPTER 7 BANKRUPTCY (DISCHARGE OF DEBTS).

As mentioned earlier, there are actually two types of bankruptcy for individuals: the discharge of debts, and the payment plan. Chapter 7 of the Bankruptcy Act is for the discharge of debts, which is the traditional bankruptcy. This is where you either pay for, or give up, your property for secured debts. You will surrender any non-exempt property in order to pay off as much of your other debt as possible. You will keep all of your other exempt property, and will be forever released from any obligation to repay the remaining debt.

C. CHAPTER 13 BANKRUPTCY (PAYMENT PLAN).

In a Chapter 13 bankruptcy you are not seeking to get rid of all of your debt entirely, but only to do one or a combination of the following:
1. Restructure your payments so that they are more manageable considering your income.
2. Get rid of part of your debt so that you can manage payments again.

This can be done by spreading your payments over a longer period of time, or by paying only a part of the loan. Either way your monthly or weekly payment will be reduced. This type of payment plan can last up to three years, which means your finances will be under the watchful eye of the trustee during this time.

The two main things the trustee and the judge will consider in deciding whether to accept your plan is whether the creditors are being treated fairly, and whether each creditor will receive at least as much as if you had gone with the traditional Chapter 7 bankruptcy.

For a Chapter 13 bankruptcy you will fill out some different forms than for a Chapter 7. The main difference is that you will need to fill out a form in which you offer a payment plan that you create. In a Chapter 13 case the creditors meeting is usually concerned with trying to reach a plan that will be acceptable to the creditors. So you may spend some time negotiating with the creditors as they try to get you to change your plan so they get more money or get it faster. It is not necessary that the creditors agree with your plan, but if they do agree it will be easily accepted by the trustee and the judge. Even if the creditors object to your plan, it will still be approved as long as it is fair (in the judge's opinion of what is fair), and as long as each creditor gets at least as much as if you had filed under Chapter 7.

It is also possible for you to convert to a Chapter 7 bankruptcy, if you later determine this is a better solution to your debt problems. It is also possible to convert a Chapter 7 to a Chapter 13 case, although this is not likely. Most people will find that they have less income to go around, therefore requiring a Chapter 7. Only if you find that your income is sufficient to enable you to pay off most of your debts within 3 years would you consider changing to a Chapter 13.

SECTION 4. DO YOU NEED A LAWYER?

In purely legal terms, the answer to this question is "No." There is no law that requires you to have a lawyer in order to file for bankruptcy. In fact, although many people have been told different, you may legally represent yourself in any type of legal proceeding.

In practical terms, if you are a middle-class wage earner, the answer is still "No." Most people are able to handle their own bankruptcy, however, you will probably need an attorney if any of the following circumstances apply in your case:
- -You are involved in a business, either yours alone or in a partnership.
- -You own stock in a privately held corporation. (This is a stock which is not available for sale to the general public. If you own such stock you will probably know what a privately held corporation is.)
- -You are married and your spouse is not filing for bankruptcy with you.
- -You are a farmer. (There are special bankruptcy laws covering farm bankruptcy).
- -You begin the procedure on your own, and encounter a creditor, trustee or judge who is particularly difficult to deal with, or a creditor who files an objection to the discharge of a debt that you think should be discharged (although you may still be able to deal with this yourself). Otherwise, a more appropriate question is posed by the next section.

A. DO YOU WANT A LAWYER?

One of your first questions about bankruptcy, and one of the reasons you are reading this book, is: How much will an attorney cost? Attorneys come in all ages, shapes, sizes, sexes, racial and ethnic groups, degrees of experience and competency— and price ranges. Most attorneys will probably charge between $750 and $1,500, depending upon where you live and how complex your case will be. If you look in the "legal services" section of the newspaper classified ads, or in the "attorneys" section of the Yellow Pages, you can probably find ads for $150 to $200 bankruptcies. These less expensive bankruptcy fees are usually available only in very simple cases, and are "no frills" services. This does not mean they are to be avoided, but be sure you know exactly what will be provided for the fee. The lawyer will usually want to be paid in advance (after all, why should he take a chance on getting paid by someone in financial trouble?).

Most new (and therefore less expensive) attorneys would be quite capable of handling a simple bankruptcy, but, if your situation became more complicated, you probably would prefer a more experienced lawyer. Also, by the time you've read this book, you will probably know as much about bankruptcy as these new attorneys.

1. SOME ADVANTAGES TO HAVING A LAWYER.
a. You may be able to save more of your property. A lawyer may be able to find more "loopholes" in the bankruptcy law, or give you other suggestions, which will preserve more assets or discharge more debt. However, these savings may be offset by

the attorney's fee you will need to pay. Generally, the more "loopholes" you want, the more experienced of an attorney you will need. And, the more experienced the attorney, the higher the attorney's fee. You're back to a cost/benefit analysis, as discussed at the beginning of this book in the INTRODUCTION TO SELF-HELP LAW BOOKS.

b. Judges and other attorneys may take you more seriously. Most judges prefer parties to a legal proceeding to have a lawyer. They feel this helps the case move in a more orderly fashion, as people who represent themselves often waste time by being unfamiliar with the procedures. However, this should not be a problem with anyone who has read this book.

c. A lawyer can serve as a "buffer" between you and your creditors. This leaves you with less stress, as your lawyer takes care of all the details.

d. Lawyers provide professional assistance with problems. In the event your case becomes complicated, it is an advantage to have an attorney who is familiar with your case. It can also be comforting to have a lawyer to turn to for advice and reassurance. Again, we come to a cost/benefit question. The more advice and reassurance, the higher the attorney's fee.

2. SOME ADVANTAGES TO REPRESENTING YOURSELF.

a. You save the cost of a lawyer.

b. Sometimes judges and trustees feel more sympathetic toward a person who is not represented by a lawyer. Often they will actually help you and protect you from lawyers for creditors.

c. The procedure may be faster. Two of the most frequent complaints about lawyers involve delay in completing the case, and failure to return phone calls. Most lawyers have heavy caseloads which can lead to cases being neglected for various periods of time. If you are following the progress of your own case, you'll be able to keep it moving through the system.

d. Selecting a good attorney is not easy. As the next section shows, it is hard to know whether you are selecting an attorney you will be happy with. The profession is blooming with lawyers who will take your money, yet provide little service in return.

3. MIDDLE GROUND.

You may want to look for an attorney who will be willing to accept an hourly fee to answer your questions and give you help on an "as needed" basis. This way you will save some legal costs but still get some professional assistance. However, beware of advertisements stating you can consult an attorney "for just twenty dollars," or "free initial consultation." Most often the attorney will simply assess your situation, tell you that he can help, and suggest that you retain him. Usually he will not actually provide you with any real usable advice, or explain how you should do something. You can probably expect to pay at least $75 per hour for such consultation.

B. SELECTING A LAWYER.

This is a two-step process. First, you need to decide which attorney to make an appointment with, then you need to decide if you want to hire that attorney.

1. FINDING POSSIBLE ATTORNEYS.
a. Ask a friend. A common, and frequently the best, way to find a lawyer is to ask someone you know to recommend one. Especially if the lawyer represented your friend in a bankruptcy or other consumer credit matter.
b. Lawyer Referral Service. You can find a referral service by looking in the Yellow Pages of your phone directory under the heading "Attorney Referral Services" or "Attorneys." In most areas such a service is provided by the local bar association, and is free of charge. It is designed to match a client with an attorney handling cases in the area of law the client needs. The referral service does not guarantee the quality of the attorney's work, nor the level of experience or ability, but it will at least connect you with a lawyer who has an interest in bankruptcy.
c. Yellow Pages. Check under the heading for "Attorneys" in the Yellow Pages phone directory. Many of the lawyers and law firms will place display ads which state their areas of practice, and some Yellow Pages have separate listings under the type of law. Look for firms or lawyers which indicate they handle bankruptcy or consumer credit matters.
d. Newspaper. Somewhere in the classified ad section you should find a section for "Legal Services." This is the best place to look if you want the least expensive attorney possible. But expect minimal services. You may even simply be given a set of forms to complete yourself!
e. Ask another lawyer. If you have used the services of an attorney in the past for some other matter (such as a will, real estate closing or traffic ticket) you may want to call and ask him to refer you to an attorney whose ability and knowledge in bankruptcy is respected.

2. EVALUATING AN ATTORNEY.
From your search you should select three to five lawyers worthy of further consideration. Your first step will be to call each attorney's office, explain that you are considering filing for bankruptcy, and ask the following questions:
        -Does the attorney (or firm) handle bankruptcies?
        -How much can you expect it to cost?
        -How soon can you get an appointment?
        -What is the cost for an initial consultation?
If you like the answers you get, ask if you can speak to the attorney. Some offices permit this, but others will require you to make an appointment. Make the appointment if that is required.
 Once you get in contact with the attorney (either by phone or at the appointment), ask the following questions:
        -How much will it cost?
        -How will the fee be paid? (Usually it is paid in advance, in full).
        -How long has the attorney been in practice?
        -What percentage of the attorney's cases involve bankruptcies? (Don't expect an exact answer, but you should get a rough estimate of at least 10%).

-How long will it take? (Don't expect an exact answer, but the attorney should be able to give you an average range and discuss things which may make a difference.

If you get acceptable answers to these questions, it's time to ASK YOURSELF these questions:

-Do I feel comfortable talking to this lawyer?
-Is this lawyer friendly toward me?
-Does this lawyer seem confident in himself?
-Does this lawyer seem willing to explain things, and able to explain things so I can understand?

If you get satisfactory answers to all of these questions, you probably have a lawyer you'll be able to work with. Most clients are happiest with an attorney they feel comfortable with. Remember, you are interviewing the lawyer to see if you want to hire him.

C. WORKING WITH AN ATTORNEY.

In general, you will work best with your attorney if you keep an open, honest and friendly attitude. You should also consider the following suggestions:

1. Ask Questions. If you want to know something, or if you don't understand something, ask your attorney. If you don't understand the answer, tell your attorney and ask him to explain it again. There are many points of law that even lawyers don't fully understand, so you shouldn't be embarrassed to ask questions. Many people who say they had a bad experience with a lawyer either didn't ask questions, or had a lawyer who wouldn't take the time to explain things. If your lawyer won't take the time to explain what he's doing, it may be time to look for a new lawyer.

2. Give Your Lawyer Complete Information. Anything you tell your lawyer is confidential. An attorney can lose his license to practice law if he reveals information without your permission. So don't hold back.

3. Accept Reality. Listen to what your lawyer tells you about the law and the system, and accept it. It will do you no good to argue because the law or the system doesn't work the way you think it should. For example, if your lawyer tells you that a hearing can't be set for another month, don't try demanding that he set one for tomorrow. Remember, it's not your lawyer's fault that the system isn't perfect, or that the law doesn't say what you'd like it to say.

4. Be Patient. Be patient with the system, as well as with your attorney. Don't expect your attorney to return your phone call within an hour. He may not be able to return it the same day either. Most lawyers are very busy, and overworked. It is rare that an attorney can maintain a full caseload and still make each client feel as if he is the only client.

5. Talk to the Secretary. Your lawyer's secretary can be a valuable source of information. So be friendly and get to know her. Often she will be able to answer your questions and you won't get a bill for the time you talk to her. Even if she can't answer your question, she can probably get the answer from the attorney and call you back faster than if you insist on waiting to speak directly to the lawyer.

6. Be On Time. This applies to appointments with your lawyer, and to court hearings.

7. Keep Your Case Moving. Many lawyers operate on the old principal of "The squeaking wheel gets the oil." Work on a case tends to get put off until a deadline is near, an emergency develops, or the client calls. There is a very good reason for this. After many years of education (and the cost of that education), lawyers hope to earn the income due a professional. This is difficult with a great many attorneys competing for clients, and the high cost of office overhead. Many lawyers find it necessary to take more cases than can be effectively handled in order to make an acceptable living. That is why many attorneys work 65 hours a week or more. Your task is to become a squeaking wheel that doesn't squeak too much. Whenever you talk to your lawyer ask him the following questions:

-What is the next step?
-When do you expect it to be done?
-When should I talk to you next?

If you don't hear from the lawyer when you expect, call him the following day. Don't remind him that he didn't call; just ask how your case is going.

PART TWO: SHOULD YOU FILE FOR BANKRUPTCY?

SECTION 5. THE EFFECTS OF BANKRUPTCY

Generally, bankruptcy should be regarded as a last resort. So, before you jump into a bankruptcy, it is a good idea to evaluate your financial situation, and consider the effects of a bankruptcy.

A. FINANCIAL EFFECTS.

A bankruptcy is a mixed blessing. It will have both positive and negative financial effects. These can be divided into immediate and long-term effects.

1. Immediate Effects.

An immediate positive effect is that your creditors will get off your back. However, this may only last a short time for certain kinds of debts. Such things as utility cut-offs, mortgage foreclosures, or evictions, may only be delayed for a few days or weeks.

Once you file for bankruptcy, your financial dealings come under the scrutiny of the bankruptcy trustee. You will need his permission to sell any assets or to pay any debts.

2. Long-Term Effects.

These are the effects after your bankruptcy is completed. The fact that you now have a bankruptcy in your history will make it difficult for you to obtain credit. This will affect your ability to qualify for a mortgage, purchase a car, or obtain a credit card. It is a long, gradual process to build up credit once you've declared bankruptcy.

You will probably also be starting over with fewer possessions than you had before your bankruptcy. Some of your property will probably get repossessed, and some of it may have to be sold.

You will have to be very careful not to get into debt problems again. You can only file for bankruptcy once every six years (this rule is a bit more complicated, and will be explained in more detail in a later Section of this book).

B. EMOTIONAL EFFECTS.

In addition to the financial effects, most people experience some emotional effects when they file for bankruptcy.

1. Yourself.

You may experience a feeling of failure or dishonesty. Failure because you couldn't manage your affairs better, or weren't smart enough to handle your money. Dishonest because you feel you are cheating your creditors. Although there are many logical arguments for not feeling this way, many people still can't overcome the feeling on an emotional level. The following categories are separate in some respects, but they are also part of how you see yourself. Regardless of how others really feel about your situation, you will see and interpret their reaction in terms of how you feel about yourself.

2. Your Family and Friends.

If you are married, your wife, and possibly your children, will have to know about the bankruptcy. You will need to prepare for how you will discuss it with them. You may also have to be prepared to deal with their feelings of failure, disappointment and guilt. There may also be extended family members involved, such as parents, brothers, aunts and uncles, and personal friends. These people may or may not understand and sympathize with your situation.

3. Your Employer.

It is possible that you can keep your bankruptcy out of your workplace, but it isn't likely. Although your employer probably won't admit it, a bankruptcy may affect your ability to obtain promotions, or to be entrusted with certain responsibilities (such as handling money or accounts). Of course the same thing may happen if you don't file, and a creditor files a wage garnishment.

For some, or all, of these reasons you should first explore whether you might avoid bankruptcy.

SECTION 6. CAN YOU AVOID BANKRUPTCY?

As you can see from the previous Section, there are some good reasons to avoid bankruptcy. There are also good reasons to file for bankruptcy, in the right circumstances. This Section will help you determine if the circumstances are right. First, we will look at your current income and expenses, then we will look at what you own and what you owe.

A. EVALUATING YOUR SITUATION: INCOME AND EXPENSES. (FORM 1)

In order to be considering bankruptcy, you must be in a situation where your income is not sufficient to cover your monthly expenses. To find out just how bad your situation is we will examine your current "budget." Make a few copies of FORM 1, found in APPENDIX A of this book, and save the original to use as a "master." Complete the INCOME AND EXPENSE STATEMENT, which is FORM 1 in APPENDIX A of this book, according to the following guidelines:
-Be sure to use MONTHLY amounts in completing this form.
-To convert a weekly amount, multiply the amount by 4.3.
-To convert a bi-weekly amount, divide by 2, then multiply the answer by 4.3.

The following relates to the INCOME portion of FORM 1:
-Take Home Pay: This refers to your total pay after you deduct for taxes and social security. If you have other payroll deductions, such as for a medical or dental plan, uniforms, or savings plan, they should be listed under the EXPENSES section of this form. Therefore, add these deductions back to the take home pay shown on your paycheck. If your pay changes from paycheck to paycheck, obtain an average by dividing your yearly income by 12, or by some other appropriate method.
-Self Employment Income: If you are self employed, either as your main job or as a second job, calculate an average monthly income. If you are self-employed and are incorporated or have employees or a financially complex business operation, consult a lawyer.
-Interest and Dividends: This includes such things as interest on bank accounts, certificates of deposit (CD's), stocks, bonds, mutual funds, etc.
-Income From Real Estate: This is income from any rental property you own.
-Retirement Income: This includes pensions and other retirement payments from your prior employment.
-Alimony or Support Payments: This includes money you receive as alimony, maintenance, child support, etc. Only count these payments if you receive them on a fairly regular and dependable basis.
-Other: This might include such things as Social Security, unemployment or disability benefits, welfare benefits, or income from loans you made to other people.

The following relates to the EXPENSES section of FORM 1:
-Homeowners/Renters Insurance: If homeowners insurance is included in your

mortgage payment, it should not be listed here again. If you rent and have renters insurance on your possessions, you will be paying it separately from your rent payment, so list it here.

   -Real Estate Taxes: If these are included in your mortgage payment, they should not be listed here again.
   -Other Installment Loan Payments: This relates to all loans except your mortgage and auto loan payments. This will include such things as credit cards, home equity loans, boat loans, vacation loans, home improvement loans, and swimming pool loans.

The remaining items are self explanatory. Just make sure everything is converted to a MONTHLY amount.

Next, add all of your monthly income and write the total in the space for TOTAL MONTHLY INCOME. Add all of your monthly expenses and write the total in the space for TOTAL MONTHLY EXPENSES. Finally, subtract the total expenses from the total income. This should give you a negative number, which will tell you how much money you are falling short by each month. (If you get a positive number, then you have either forgotten to list some of your expenses, or you are making enough money to meet your monthly expenses and should not be thinking about bankruptcy.)

B. EVALUATING YOUR SITUATION: ASSETS AND DEBTS

To put it simply, an "asset" is something you own (such as money, a house, a car, furniture, etc.), and a "debt" is money you owe. The two things you will consider in trying to avoid bankruptcy are whether you can cut your expenses, and whether you can sell some assets and pay off some debts. But before we can get into all of that, it is necessary to explain the types of property and debts involved in a bankruptcy. Then, we will discuss some general guidelines for determining whether bankruptcy is right for you. Finally, we will discuss what can be done to try to avoid bankruptcy.

1. TYPES OF DEBTS.

In a bankruptcy, debts are first divided into two types: "dischargeable" and "non-dischargeable." A "dischargeable" debt is one which the bankruptcy laws allow you to discharge, or cancel. The best example of a dischargeable debt is the money you owe on credit cards, such as a VISA, Mastercard, or department store card. Most consumer debts are dischargeable in bankruptcy, and these are the types of debts that lead most people into a situation which requires them to file for bankruptcy. If you have several credit cards, and you charge them all up to the limit, it is easy to get in over your head. It is easy to recall cases in which an individual, or more often a young couple, have charged as much as $15,000. And that was in addition to their mortgage payment and car payment!

A non-dischargeable debt is one which you will still owe after the bankruptcy is completed. Examples of non-dischargeable debts are:
   -Student loans.
   -Child support or alimony obligations.
   -Delinquent taxes.

-Some court-ordered judgments.
-Debts arising from fraud (such as from providing
false credit application information, from theft,
or from obtaining credit with the intention of
filing for bankruptcy to avoid payment).

Debts are also divided into two other categories: "secured" and "unsecured." A secured debt is one which can be viewed as "attached" to a particular piece of property. The prime example of a secured debt is a mortgage. The mortgage means that, if you don't pay the money you borrowed to buy your house, the lender can take your house. Most car loans also include a "financing statement," which is essentially the same as a mortgage. If you don't pay, the lender gets your car.

However, most credit card loans are unsecured. They are not tied to any particular piece of property. If you don't pay, the bank can't grab your property (at least not without going to all of the trouble of suing you and trying to attach your property later).

You will later complete a Property and Debt Inventory form which will divide your debts according to these categories. Generally, the more "dischargeable" and "unsecured" debts you have, the more a bankruptcy will be helpful to you.

2. TYPES OF PROPERTY.

Just as debts are divided into categories, so is your property. Property is divided into "exempt" and "non-exempt" categories.

Remember, the purpose of bankruptcy is to help you start over financially. It wouldn't help to leave you with absolutely no property, so the bankruptcy laws allow you to keep a certain amount of your property. The types and amounts of property you are allowed to keep are "exempt" property. What type and amount of property is exempt is a matter of state law. Although the bankruptcy act is a federal law, the question of exempt property is determined by your state government. Generally, most states exempt the following types of property, at least up to a certain value or amount:
-Motor vehicles.
-Clothing and personal effects.
-Household furnishings.
-Tools used in your trade or profession.
-Equity in a home.
-Life insurance.
-Public employee pensions.
-Social Security, welfare, unemployment or workers' compensation, or other
public benefits accumulated in a bank account.
Typical examples of non-exempt property are:
-The above items over a certain amount.
-A Second car.
-A Boat or recreational vehicle.
-A Vacation home.
-Cash, bank accounts, certificates of deposit.
-Other investments, such as stocks, bonds, coin collections, etc.

The Property and Debt Inventory form you will soon fill out will divide your property into exempt and non-exempt categories.

> CAUTION: Even if the property is exempt, you may still lose the property if it is tied to a secured debt. For example: Your home is exempt property under your state's laws. If you borrowed money from a bank to buy the house, and the bank holds a mortgage on the house, the bank can still foreclose and take your house if you don't pay.

C. PROPERTY AND DEBT INVENTORY. (FORMS 2 and 3).

Now you will complete the PROPERTY INVENTORY (FORM 2), and the DEBT INVENTORY (FORM 3), which may be found in Appendix A of this book.

1. PROPERTY INVENTORY (FORM 2).

The PROPERTY INVENTORY (FORM 2 in APPENDIX A of this book) is divided into six columns, each of which has both a number and a title. The following instructions refer to each column by number.

In column (1), list all of your property. Do not list anything in more than one category. For each category, turn to the listing for your state in APPENDIX B of this book. For each category of property in FORM 2, check if any such items are exempt on your state's list. If so, be sure to list those items separately. For example, if your state exempts "wedding rings," be sure to list your wedding rings as a separate item in the "Jewelry" category in FORM 2. You should also compare your state's exemptions with the federal exemptions at the beginning of APPENDIX B, if you live in one of the states which permit the federal exemptions as an alternative to the state exemptions. These states are listed at the beginning of APPENDIX B. Also Column (1) is divided into several categories of property, as follows:

-Real Estate: List any real estate you own, by each property's address or other brief description.
-Autos: Include cars, trucks, motorcycles, etc.
-Boats: Include boats, engines, boating equipment, as well as any other recreational vehicles.
-Cash on hand: This is cash in your pocket, wallet, purse, mattress, etc. It does not include money in a bank.
-Bank accounts: This is where you list all of your bank accounts, by your bank name and account number.
-Clothing: You can just give an estimate of the total value of your clothing. Only list specific items if they have great value (such as a mink coat, or original designer items).
-Jewelry: Costume jewelry need not be listed by item, but gold, diamonds and other precious metals and gems should be listed by each item.
-Household goods: This includes all of your furniture, pots and pans, dishes, personal items, etc. A general estimate can be given for most things, although any items of great value should be listed separately, but first check to see it they fit in one of the other categories in this form.

-Collections: This is for such things as coins, stamps, paintings, books, and other valuable collectibles.

-Sports equipment: This includes firearms, pool tables, golf clubs, etc.

-Business goods/Trade tools: This includes any such items you need in order to conduct your business or to engage in your occupation.

-Investments: This includes any stocks, bonds, patents, copyrights, licenses, etc.

-Insurance: This includes any cash value in life insurance policies, annuities, etc.

-Other property: This is where you list anything which doesn't fit into one of the other categories. Again, be sure to check your state's listing in APPENDIX B.

Column (2) is titled "VALUE." Fill in the approximate value of each of the items of property you listed under Column (1). For some items you will know the exact value, and for others you will have to make a good estimate. For such things as autos and boats you may be able to find a "blue book" (which may actually be any color) at your local library or at a local dealer, which will give approximate values. For other items, such as clothing, personal belongings and furniture, just estimate what you think you could sell these items for at a garage sale. Estimate low, but don't get ridiculous.

Column (3) is used to fill in how much money, if any, you still owe on any of the items listed under Column (1). For the purposes of this form, you only "owe" something if the item can be foreclosed on or repossessed if you fail to pay. For example, if you purchased your dining set with your VISA card, it can't be repossessed, therefore, you don't owe anything on the dining set. Next, subtract the amount owed in Column (3) from the value in Column (2), and write in the difference in Column (4). This will give you your equity in each piece of property. "Equity" is the amount of cash you would have if you sold the property and paid off the amount you owe.

Column (5) is completed by referring to your state's listing in Appendix B of this book. Under the listing for your state you will find a list of the items and amounts that are exempt. Also look at the beginning of APPENDIX B to see if you are in a state which permits you to use the federal bankruptcy exemptions. If so, you need to compare the state and federal exemptions to see which would make more of your property exempt. In most cases the state exemptions will give you a better result, but not always. If you will get more exempt property under the federal exemptions, use them instead of the state exemptions. With respect to each item of property, you may find that item to be completely exempt, or that only part of its value is exempt. The following examples will help illustrate this point (assuming you have no mortgage on your home):

-EXAMPLE 1: If you live in Florida, the home you live in is completely exempt, no matter what its value. If you have a home worth $100,000, it is fully exempt. This means you don't have to sell your house to pay off your creditors. (But if you have a mortgage, you have to make your payments).

-EXAMPLE 2: If you live in Illinois, only $7,500 of the value of your home is exempt. If your home is worth $100,000, you may only claim an exemption of $7,500. This means you would have to sell your home, or take out a new mortgage for $92,500 so that your equity is only $7,500. Of course you would have to keep up your mortgage payments, if you could get such a loan with your current financial problems.

-EXAMPLE 3: If you live in New Jersey, your home is not exempt at all. Whether your equity is $100,000 or $1.00 you would lose it in a bankruptcy.

So, look at your state's listing in Appendix B and determine what is exempt for each item of property. Fill in the amount of the exemption in Column (5).

In Column (6), place a check mark beside each item of property for which the debt is "secured." (If necessary, re-read part B.1 in this Section on secured and unsecured debts). If the debt for that property is secured, you will need to keep up your payment, or at least work out something with the creditor, in order to keep the property (even if the property is exempt in your state).

2. DEBT INVENTORY (FORM 3).

Next, complete the DEBT INVENTORY (FORM 3 in APPENDIX A of this book) according to the following guidelines.

This form is divided into six columns, five of which are numbered. The first column is to help remind you of the types of property you have. In Column (1) list each debt you owe by the name of the lender and the account number.

In Column (2) list what the loan was for, such as home, car, boat, vacation, etc. For your credit cards you don't need to list each little purchase you made, as the only purpose of this column is to help you remember what the loan is for, and to determine whether the loan is secured by any property.

In Column (3) write down the balance due on each loan. You don't need to have each one exact "to the penny," but be as accurate as possible.

In Column (4) write in the same amount as Column (3) for each loan which is secured by a piece of property. If necessary, go back to part B.1 of this Section which explains "secured" and "unsecured" debts.

In Column (5) write in the same amount as Column (3) for each loan that is a dischargeable loan. For purposes of FORM 3, a secured loan is not considered dischargeable, unless you are willing to give up that item of property. Again, refer to part B.1 of this Section which explains "dischargeable" and "non-dischargeable" loans.

D. GENERAL GUIDELINES.

In order to determine whether you should file for bankruptcy, you need to evaluate you situation according to the following four factors:

1. Can you reduce your total monthly payments so that you can manage things on your income?

2. How much of your debt is dischargeable?

3. How much of your debt is secured by your property?

4. How much of your property is exempt?

Once you have done this, you can get a good idea of whether you can avoid bankruptcy and where things would stand after a bankruptcy. You will be able to estimate how much property you would be able to keep, and how much money you would still owe to creditors.

Let's look at your monthly budget first (FORM 1). Examine each of your monthly expenses. Are there any that you can reduce or eliminate? Can you sell some of your property to pay off some of your debts? Can you move to a cheaper apartment, or sell your home and find an apartment which will reduce your monthly housing costs? Can you sell your late model car and buy a less expensive one? This is no time to think about maintaining your lifestyle. After all, it may be your lifestyle that got you into financial trouble in the first place! If you can make such adjustments to your expenses, you may be able to avoid bankruptcy. If such adjustments still won't help your situation, continue on to the next paragraph and look at the types of debts and property you have.

A general rule of thumb is that if you can discharge more than 50% of your debts, a Chapter 7 bankruptcy would probably improve your financial situation. To determine if your situation fits this guideline, refer to FORM 3, take the total of Column (3) and divide it by 2. If the answer is equal to or less than the total of Column (5), you can probably benefit from a Chapter 7 bankruptcy. If the answer is greater than the total of Column (5), you may benefit from a Chapter 13 bankruptcy, or even avoid bankruptcy.

SECTION 7. ALTERNATIVES TO BANKRUPTCY

If, after filling out FORMS 1, 2 and 3 from APPENDIX A of this book, it looks like you may be able to avoid bankruptcy, this Section will present some ideas for how you can get your debt problems under control.

A. CREDIT COUNSELING.

If you would like to avoid either type of bankruptcy, you may want to see a credit counselor.

WARNING: Beware of private "debt counselors" or offers for "debt consolidation" loans. Such "help" often only results in one large payment instead of many smaller payments, and you will still have trouble making that monthly payment. Furthermore, such operations charge counseling fees which only further take away needed cash. Soon you will be facing bankruptcy again. Also, AVOID the now-famous "home equity loan." This can end up converting your unsecured debts into secured debts, which means that you can't file for bankruptcy without losing your home!

You can feel comfortable going to see a credit counselor who is associated with your local Consumer Credit Counseling Service. This organization can be found in the Yellow Pages telephone directory under the heading "Credit Counseling." This is a non-profit organization set up by creditors, such as banks, department stores, credit card companies and other businesses. A credit counselor will contact your creditors, help establish new payment arrangements, and help you set up a budget you can handle. However, if you miss payments on your new budget, you may still end up in a bankruptcy and will have possibly paid hundreds of dollars to your creditors. In this situation, it would have been better for you to have filed for bankruptcy at the start.

A Consumer Credit Counseling (CCC) plan is similar to a Chapter 13 bankruptcy, but is on a less formal basis. It is also cheaper, in that the cost of the CCC assistance is minimal (about $20.00), whereas higher court filing fees and other costs are involved in a Chapter 13 case. It may look better on a credit report to have a record of CCC assistance, than to have a record of a bankruptcy. The main financial difference is that a CCC plan will require you to pay your debts in full, whereas a Chapter 13 may only require payment of a portion of your debts.

If you feel a strong obligation to pay your creditors in full, you should consider paying a visit to your local Consumer Credit Counseling Service office.

B. BE YOUR OWN CREDIT COUNSELOR.

In theory, there is nothing a credit counselor can do that you can't do. On a practical level, some creditors may be more inclined to listen to a credit counselor, although they should pay just as much attention to you. Your creditors don't want you to file for bankruptcy, because it means they won't get paid in full. So they should have a strong incentive to be reasonable. Your main goal is to get the creditor to allow you to make smaller payments, over a longer period of time.

For example, George has a $1,500 balance on a credit card from a local department store. His payments are $74.89 a month, and the balance will take two years to pay off. If the department store will agree to accept payments over an additional year, George's monthly payment will be lowered to $54.23 a month. This lowers his monthly payment by $20.66. If he has ten loans like this, he could save over $200 per month, which may be enough to enable him to keep up his payments based on his income.

1. PLANNING A BUDGET.

The place to begin is by reviewing a fresh copy of FORM 1, the INCOME AND EXPENSE STATEMENT you completed earlier. You will need this form and a calculator to plan your budget. (If you don't have a calculator or adding machine, you'll just have to do the arithmetic by hand). The copy of FORM 1 you just completed shows your budget as it is right now. Use the fresh copy to start your new budget. Your total income will remain the same, so write it in under TOTAL MONTHLY INCOME. Now enter this amount in your calculator. We will now go through all of your expenses, and will subtract each one from the total income figure. First, identify the most important item, which is probably your rent or mortgage payment (unless you are prepared to go live with friends and relatives). Write this amount in the appropriate place on the form, and subtract it from your total income.

Next, identify your next most important expense, and so on. For each item, ask yourself if there is any way to reduce the amount you spend each month. If you can reduce the amount, use the reduced amount, and subtract it from the total. Your absolutely essential payments are for housing (including utilities), food, and transportation (probably your car). In order to survive and earn a living, you need a place to live, food, and a way to get to and from work. If you are unable to make these essential payments on your income, or are unable to reduce these payments to that level, you may want to apply for some kind of public assistance (yes, welfare) in addition to filing for a Chapter 7 bankruptcy.

Once you have subtracted the essential living expenses, you will be left with the total remaining income available to pay your creditors and other expenses. (Absolutely last on your list should be the "Recreation/Travel/Entertainment" expenses). Now, start subtracting your payments for loans that are "secured" loans. These are any loans where your property can be repossessed if you don't pay. Most credit card debts are not secured by any particular property. The most common secured loans are for homes (including home equity loans), automobiles, boats, and occasionally furniture. If the only paper you signed was the typical charge card receipt for VISA, Mastercard, Sears, or other department store charges, the loan is not secured.

By now you are probably left with a small amount of income left (if any at all), with which you can make payments on the rest of your loans. Add up the remaining loan payments, and subtract them from your remaining income. If your answer is -0- or more, whatever adjustments you made to your expenses were enough to eliminate your debt problem. Now your only problem is to try to live according to your new budget.

If your answer is less than -0-, however, this is how much you need to reduce your monthly payments in order to avoid having to file for bankruptcy. Your next step is to try to convince your creditors to adjust your payments to fit your remaining income.

2. DEALING WITH CREDITORS.

Your next task is to create a new payment plan to present to your unsecured creditors. What you need to come up with is a plan that is fair to all of your creditors. For your unsecured creditors, you will want to reduce each payment by a proportional amount. First, take the total monthly payments of your remaining debts, and divide it by the monthly shortage. This will give you the percentage you need to reduce each debt by in order to match your remaining income. For example, Sue has subtracted all of her essential expenses and secured loan payments from her income, and is left with $245.00. She has five monthly credit card payments as follows:

-VISA	$150.00
-Mastercard	65.00
-Sears	50.00
-Discovery	23.00
-Local department store	75.00
TOTAL PAYMENTS	$363.00

Sue's income is $118 short ($363 - 245 = 118). If she divides the amount she is short (118) by the total payments (363), she gets a figure of .325, which she will round up to .33 (or just about one-third). If she reduces each payment by .33 she will have enough income to meet the new payments. To find the amount to reduce each payment by, Sue will multiply each payment amount by .33, round off each answer, and then subtract this amount from each payment:

CREDITOR	OLD PAY.	SUBTRACT	NEW PAY.
VISA	$150.00	$50.00	$100.00
Mastercard	65.00	21.50	43.50
Sears	50.00	16.50	33.50
Discovery	23.00	7.50	15.50
Local Dept. Store	75.00	25.00	50.00
TOTALS	363.00	120.50	242.50

As you can see, Sue has lowered her payments to fit her income, and has treated each creditor the same. If she can convince these creditors to accept the lower payments, she has her new budget (and she has an extra $2.50 left over!). Of course this will increase the number of payments needed to pay off the loans.

Once you've worked out your new proposed payment amounts it is time to contact your creditors with your plan. You will contact them by way of a letter. FORM 19 in APPENDIX A of this book is a form letter you can use. Just fill in the blanks according to your new payment plan, fill in your name and address (so it can be read), sign your name and mail a copy to each creditor. Be sure to type in your name, address and account number below your signature. It is a good idea to send these letters by certified, return-receipt mail. This will cost you a couple of dollars per letter, but you will later be able to prove the creditor received it if you need to. Now you sit back and wait for your creditors to answer. Be sure to fill in the return receipt number from the white receipt on both the green card and in the blank at the top of the letter (FORM 19). You will note that the form letter states that your next payment will be according to the new schedule unless you hear from the creditor beforehand.

You may be asking, "Why should the creditor accept reduced payments?" If the creditor really believes you are serious about bankruptcy, and sees that you have a workable budget, he has every reason to accept your plan. His alternative is to let you declare bankruptcy, in which case he will receive absolutely nothing.

You should try to get your unsecured creditors to lower their payment requirements in order to fit your budget. Only after this fails should you contact your secured creditors about a new payment schedule. Now you may wonder why a secured creditor would agree to lower payments, when all he has to do is repossess or foreclose. Even a secured creditor would rather get paid than take back the property. It takes a lot of time and expense to repossess and resell property. And if you do file for bankruptcy it will take even more time and expense. A bankruptcy won't stop foreclosure, but it will delay it. Therefore, most lenders will work with you to try to avoid repossession or bankruptcy. The key to success is showing the creditor a fair and reasonable payment plan that is clearly within your ability to maintain. And you can still go to credit counseling, as discussed at the beginning of this chapter.

If this doesn't resolve your problem, you may need to proceed to the next Section of this book to prepare for filing for bankruptcy.

PART THREE: PREPARATION FOR BANKRUPTCY

SECTION 8. ARRANGING YOUR FINANCES

WARNING: USE THIS SECTION WITH EXTREME CAUTION. Before you file for bankruptcy, you may want to review your financial situation to see if there is anything you can rearrange to your advantage. Before we discuss various such ideas, you need to be aware that you may be walking a fine line between acceptable practices and what the court might consider to be cheating your creditors. At a very minimum, you should not file for bankruptcy for at least 90 days after you make any of the changes discussed in this Section, and if any changes involve a relative, you should not file for at least one year. However, each bankruptcy judge has his own ideas and attitudes, and some have determined that there was an intent to defraud where transfers were made more than a year before filing!

Now let's look at some things you might do before you file which will improve your situation after your bankruptcy is complete.

A. SELL NON-EXEMPT PROPERTY AND BUY EXEMPT PROPERTY.

The most obvious thing you might do is sell non-exempt property, and use the money to buy exempt property. For example, if you live in New York, furniture, a radio, TV, refrigerator, and clothing are exempt. However, a boat or second car is not exempt. Therefore, you may want to sell your boat or second car, and use the money you get to buy some furniture, a radio, TV, refrigerator, or some clothing. If you are like most people, furniture or clothing are probably your best bet, because you already have a radio, TV and refrigerator. You will need to carefully read the list of exemptions for your state in APPENDIX B of this book.

B. SELL NON-EXEMPT PROPERTY AND PAY SOME DEBTS.

Generally, you want to sell non-exempt property, and use the money to pay off either a non-dischargeable debt (such as a student loan or overdue taxes), or pay off a secured debt on exempt property (such as making that overdue mortgage payment).

EXAMPLE 1. You have a non-exempt boat. You sell it and use the money to pay off a student loan. In the bankruptcy you would lose the boat anyway, so you may as well use it to reduce the number of payments you'll need to make after bankruptcy on your non-dischargeable debts.

EXAMPLE 2. You have a non-exempt second car. You sell it and use the money to pay off the balance on the loan for your primary car, which is exempt in your state. You get to keep your primary car after bankruptcy, and you will have one less payment to make (provided your primary car isn't worth more than the allowable exemption).

CAUTION: Be sure you don't pay off a loan on a non-exempt piece of property, because you will lose the property in bankruptcy anyway. EXAMPLE: You sell your second car and use the money to pay off your secured boat loan. The boat, being non-exempt property, is then taken by the trustee, sold, and used to pay off other unsecured creditors. You have gained nothing.

You may also want to sell non-exempt property to pay off an unsecured loan. Paying an unsecured loan will only be of advantage under one or both of the following circumstances:

1. A friend or relative has co-signed the loan and you don't want to "stick" that friend or relative with having to pay the loan for you.

2. You want to maintain good relations with that particular creditor, and be able to keep your ability to buy there on credit.

C. DEFRAUDING CREDITORS. (DON'T!)

Rearranging your asset and debt situation can get you into trouble. If it appears to the court that you have made changes in order to cheat your creditors, the judge can let the trustee take and sell the new property you've purchased, or he can even dismiss your case and not let you have a discharge of any debts. This will leave you in a much worse situation than you began with.

In order to minimize the chances of problems, keep the following points in mind:

1. Don't make so many sales that you would have enough money to pay off most or all of your debts (unless this is your goal in order to avoid bankruptcy). If you sell enough property to be able to pay off your debts, and don't pay them off, it will be considered fraud.

2. Sell and buy property at market value prices. If you sell something for far less than a reasonable or market price, or buy something for far more that it is worth, your creditors may object.

3. Avoid sales to, or purchases from, relatives. Do it if absolutely necessary, but be sure you make the exchange at market value.

4. Don't sell something expensive and buy something cheap, planning to secretly pocket the cash. The judge or trustee can make you account for all of the cash you get from a sale, and either you come up with the extra cash or get your case dismissed.

5. If the trustee, judge or creditors ask you about your transactions before you filed, just tell the truth. One of the main things the court will consider in deciding if your action was fraud is your intention. If you freely admit that you did adjust your property so you could get a better start after the bankruptcy, it will be seen as an indication that you didn't intend to defraud your creditors. Furthermore, if you are asked about a particular transaction, you can be sure that the person asking the questions already knows about it. Judges don't like people who lie or are sneaky (except other lawyers of course), so don't try to hide things. You are bound to get caught.

6. Don't buy more non-exempt property on credit, then sell the items to buy exempt property. This is fraud.

7. Don't go overboard and sell all of your non-exempt property. Leave something for the unsecured creditors so they don't feel cheated and challenge the transactions.

SECTION 9. GATHERING INFORMATION

Before you start preparing any forms, you will need to gather information about your finances. You should already have most, if not all, of the information you need. Your petition for bankruptcy will consist mostly of describing your financial situation at a certain point in time. You will need to gather together all of your papers regarding your income, monthly expenses, assets and debts.

This information will be necessary for you to adequately fill out the forms to file for bankruptcy, and will also be useful in the event a judge, creditor or trustee asks you how you came up with the figures on your forms. The following comments regarding the type of information you need should answer any questions you have.

A. INCOME.

For most people, income information will come from three primary sources: Paystubs, tax returns, and W-2 statements. Your paystub should give the most current information. Look for a space that shows your "Year to Date," or "YTD" income. This will give your total earnings since the beginning of the current year. You can then count up the number of weeks or months that have passed since January 1st, and divide that into your year to date earnings to get an average weekly or monthly amount. If your paystub doesn't show a year to date figure, you can always add up the totals of all paystubs since the beginning of the year.

Another good source of income information is your previous year's income tax return, or W-2 statement. This information will be useable as long as you didn't get a raise, change jobs, or have any other change in income.

If you have additional income from such things as bank account interest, stock dividends, alimony, etc., get out any statements or other records which show this income.

If you have income from self-employment, you should gather your accounting records and tax returns.

B. EXPENSES.

Basically you should get out any papers or records which show how much your monthly expenses are. This should include at least the following:

1. HOUSING EXPENSE. If you have a mortgage, you probably have a payment book which shows your monthly payment. If not, look for cancelled checks to the mortgage holder, a copy of the note and mortgage showing the payment, an escrow statement showing the amount withheld each month for taxes and insurance, or some similar record. If you rent, you should have a copy of a lease which shows the monthly rent, or at least cancelled checks or receipts. If you can't find any of these, ask your

mortgage company or landlord to send you a statement to verify the amount of your payment.

2. UTILITIES. Get out your monthly statements for your electric, gas, telephone, trash pick-up, and any other utility bill. Hopefully you've kept at least the last couple of bills. If not, be sure to keep the next one that comes. You could also write to the utility company and ask for a month-by-month statement for the past year (this information may actually be on some of your bills).

3. FOOD. This will not be as easy to find documentation for, as most people don't keep their sales receipts for food. However, if you normally write a check for your food shopping you can get an average from your checkbook information. If you can't find any such information, you probably still have a pretty good idea of about how much you spend on food for a week or month.

4. LOAN PAYMENTS. This information should be easy to find, in the form of a monthly statement or payment book. For credit cards you should get a monthly billing statement, which will give the balance owed and the minimum monthly payment. For other debts, such as auto loans, you will probably have a payment book.

5. OTHER DEBTS. This includes such things as insurance premiums, gas and maintenance expenses for your car, child day care, and any other expenses. Some of these items will have some sort of documentation and some you will simply have to estimate. This information should already be on the INCOME AND EXPENSE STATEMENT (FORM 1) you prepared earlier.

C. ASSETS.

This is figuring out what you own. At this point we are not concerned with how much you owe, or what it is worth. Your list will include items such as the following:

1. REAL ESTATE. A deed or mortgage will sufficiently describe the property, by way of a legal description. You will probably only need the street address, but it's a good idea to have the legal description on hand.

2. VEHICLES. You will need the year, make and model of each vehicle you own. You probably already know this information, but it's a good idea to have some paperwork on hand, such as the title, bill of sale, registration, or loan papers.

3. BANK ACCOUNTS, ETC. You will need copies of your most current statements, or other records, showing the current balance in all checking and savings accounts, certificates of deposit (CD's), IRA accounts, etc.

4. OTHER "FINANCIAL" ASSETS. This includes such things as stocks and bonds, mutual funds, annuities, life insurance policies with a cash value, and any kind of retirement account or fund. All of these things should have some kind of statement or other paperwork to show current values.

5. JEWELRY AND OTHER COLLECTIBLES. These items will probably not have any papers to document their value, unless you've had the item appraised or insured for a certain amount, or have borrowed money to purchase the item. (Unless you still happen to have the receipt for an item which hasn't gone up in value much since you bought it). Where there is no documentation, just make a list of the items, and write down your estimate of what you could sell it for.

6. OTHER PERSONAL BELONGINGS. This category includes all of your furniture, clothing, pots, pans and dishes, and other everyday personal possessions. Of course, if any of these items are especially valuable, you need to treat them the same as jewelry and collectibles. Otherwise, just make a note in each category with an amount you think it would cost to replace the entire category. It is not necessary for you to list each piece of clothing, or each pot and pan, separately.

D. DEBTS.

Your most likely debts are a mortgage, auto loan and credit cards. A "debt" will have an outstanding balance, and almost certainly an interest rate. This distinguishes a debt from other monthly obligations such as rent and utility payments. There will also be either a monthly statement or payment book, and probably some other paperwork you completed or received when you first obtained the credit. Mainly, you will need to know the name and address of who the money is owed to, the account number, and the amount owed.

E. LEGAL RESEARCH.

As the law is subject to change at any time, it is strongly suggested that you review your state's exemption laws before you file. The best place to do this is at a law library, and the best place to find such a library is at your local courthouse. Law schools also have good law libraries. There are two main sources of information: (1) your state's laws, which are named in your state's exemptions in APPENDIX B of this book, and (2) the "Bankruptcy Reporter," which is a nationwide collection of the decisions of the various bankruptcy courts. If you find an "annotated" set of laws for your state, they will also refer to significant court decisions.

State laws are most often referred to as "statutes" or "codes", and contain the exact law as passed by your state legislature. The laws are identified by numbers called "titles," "chapters" or "sections," depending upon your state's system. A few states (namely Maryland, New York and Texas) further complicate things by first breaking the laws down by subject, then breaking each subject down into sections. Once you find the particular law relating to your exemption, read the exact language to be sure there aren't any special qualifications required for the exemption.

If you can't find the law you need in the main volume, there is another place you can look. All of the states periodically update their statutes. Some states do this by a paperback supplement which slides into a pocket in the back of the hard-cover volume. Other states publish either a hard-cover or a paperback volume, which you can find as the last book of the series of laws. Be sure to check the supplement.

Many states also have sets of laws which are "annotated." This means that, after each law is stated, there is more information to help you understand what the law means. This includes brief summaries of court decisions interpreting that law. The supplements will also be annotated, which is where you will find the most recent information.

The "Bankruptcy Reporter" is a multi-volume set of books which contain significant court decisions in bankruptcy cases. In most cases, you will only be concerned with the more recent, paperback volumes. You will want to look at the index section, in the front of each volume, which will contain a summary of the court decisions. Look for the decisions from your state, which is abbreviated at the beginning of each summary.

If you really want to study the details of bankruptcy law, take a look at the volumes on bankruptcy by "Collier." Your law library will probably have a section of shelves devoted to bankruptcy books. This is where you will find Collier's, the Bankruptcy Reporter, and other books about bankruptcy. These books will contain additional forms, as well as detailed information.

If you have any difficulty, ask the librarian for assistance. However, don't expect the librarian to give you any legal advice.

worry about any amounts owed, or whether the property is subject to any exemption. Total Column (3).

7. SCHEDULE B-4: PROPERTY CLAIMED AS EXEMPT.

At the top of the page, you need to check whether you are selecting the federal exemptions or your state's exemptions. The federal exemptions are only available in certain states, which are listed at the beginning of APPENDIX B. If available in your state, you will need to compare the exemptions available in your state with the federal exemptions (both sets of exemptions are found in APPENDIX B of this book), and see which set will allow you to keep more of your property. If you select the state exemptions, you need to fill in the name of your state. If you select the state exemptions, you may also use the Federal Non-Bankruptcy Exemptions, found near the beginning of APPENDIX B of this book.

To complete this part, refer to Column (5) of FORM 2, where you have already identified the items you are claiming as exempt. You may want to once again consult the information in APPENDIX B of this book relating to your state to be sure you are claiming everything to which you may be entitled. If you aren't sure whether you can claim an item, claim it! Let the trustee or a creditor question it. (Of course, don't claim something you know is clearly not exempt, but if you genuinely aren't sure give yourself the benefit of the exemption).

In Column (1) fill in the type of property. Try to use the same categories as those for your state in APPENDIX B. In Column (2) type in where the property is located, and a description of the property. If most or all of the property is at your home, you can make a notation at the top of Column (2) that: "Unless otherwise indicated, all property is located at debtor's residence."

In Column (3) state the statute or law which gives you the exemption you are claiming. Again, refer to APPENDIX B of this book for the statute number. Examples of how to cite these laws appear at the beginning of each state's exemption listing. Column (4) is to state the value of the exempt property. Be sure you are not exceeding the maximum amount of the exemption allowed as indicated in APPENDIX B. Total Column (4).

8. SUMMARY OF DEBTS AND PROPERTY.

This is the last part of FORM 7, and is simply a summary of the other parts. The far left column lists the items from the various parts of FORM 7. Go back and look at the same item in the appropriate part of FORM 7, and fill in the proper amount in each column. If any of the items do not apply, type "N/A" on the corresponding line. Do not leave any lines blank. Then complete the Unsworn Declaration Under Penalty of Perjury at the bottom of the page, by typing your name (and your spouse's name if appropriate), the number of sheets of paper making up FORM 7 (including any extra sheets you attached), and by dating and signing the form.

D. SCHEDULE OF CURRENT INCOME AND EXPENDITURES (FORM 8).

The previous form states what you own and what you owe. This form states what you earn and what you spend. Part A of the form asks for information about your family status, and is self-explanatory. Part B asks for information about your employment. Questions 1 and 2 of part B are directed to your situation, and questions 3 and 4 are directed to your spouse (only if you are married, of course). Once again, if either you or your spouse are self-employed, you should probably consult an attorney.

To complete parts C and D, refer to FORM 1 which you filled out earlier. The only thing you need to do is separate your income information between what you earn, and what your spouse earns. Note the instruction at the bottom of part C, asking you to attach an additional sheet of paper explaining your situation if you are expecting to receive some income in the next six months which is not a monthly payment. Some examples would be a tax refund, or an inheritance. Also note the instruction at the bottom of part D, asking you to attach an additional sheet with an explanation if you expect any large change in your expenses in the near future. For example, a car loan you are about to make your last payment on, alimony you will begin paying once your divorce is final, or medical bills you will soon begin making payments on.

Complete the Unsworn Declaration Under Penalty of Perjury at the bottom of the form.

E. STATEMENT OF FINANCIAL AFFAIRS FOR DEBTOR NOT ENGAGED IN BUSINESS (FORM 9).

This is another lengthy form, but one which is not difficult to complete because the instructions are rather clear and simple. All you need to do is read each question in the first column, and type in the answers in the second and third columns. If the answer to any question is "none", write that in the space. If the answer is "not applicable," write in "N/A". Do not leave any questions unanswered. Some of the questions may require you to go back through your records for the past few years. Just answer the questions as best you can, with the information you can recall or locate.

Question 3a asks you where you filed your tax returns for the past two years. An example would be "IRS, Atlanta, Georgia." Question 5c asks you to explain if any of your financial records are not available. This only needs to be answered if you answered "yes" to question 5a. In other words, if you never kept any books or records, you don't need to answer question 5c. The same applies to question 5d.

Questions 6 and 7 ask about property owned by one person, but held by another. Question 6 concerns property you are holding for another person. This is to protect that person's property from being sold as part of your bankruptcy. Of course, an easier way

SECTION 12: PAYMENT PLAN PROCEDURE
(CHAPTER 13 BANKRUPTCY)

This Section will give you line-by-line instructions for filling out the forms necessary for a Chapter 13 bankruptcy, or "wage earner plan." For this procedure you may need to fill out some of the same forms that are used in a Chapter 7 bankruptcy. Where this is the case, you will be referred to the appropriate instructions in Section 11 of this book.

A. THE PETITION. (FORM 5).

The following instructions relate to FORM 5 in APPENDIX A of this book, which is entitled "VOLUNTARY PETITION--CHAPTER 13." Be sure you are using FORM 5, because FORM 4 is titled "VOLUNTARY PETITION--CHAPTER 7," but it is only for a Chapter 7 bankruptcy.

This is a very simple form to complete. Fill in the top portion of the form according to the instructions in Section 10 of this book. Type your address, including your county, on the line in paragraph 1 of the form. An example would be "426 Fourth Street, Phoenix, Maricopa County, Arizona."

Next, fill in the date on the line in paragraph 4. This refers to the date of your Chapter 13 Plan, which you will prepare later in this Section. You can use the date you expect to file your petition, or you can wait until you have everything ready to file then come back and fill in the date. Certain time requirements are based on the date you file, so you don't want to be using a date in your petition which is earlier than your filing date.

Finally, type in the date on the line at the bottom of the form, and sign your name where indicated. If you are married and are filing the petition together, your spouse will also need to sign. Be sure to read the entire Voluntary Petition so that you know what you are signing.

Along with your Voluntary Petition, you will need to file other various documents, depending upon your situation. Each of these documents is discussed and explained below.

B. APPLICATION AND ORDER TO PAY FILING FEE IN INSTALLMENTS. (FORM 6).

Complete this form according to the instructions in Section 11, part B of this book.

C. STATEMENT OF FINANCIAL AFFAIRS FOR DEBTOR NOT ENGAGED IN BUSINESS (FORM 9).

Complete this form according to the instructions in Section 11, part E of this book. This is a long form, with many sub-parts, so be sure you complete the entire form.

D. CHAPTER 13 STATEMENT (FORM 12).

This lengthy form is the central document to a Chapter 13 bankruptcy. It combines, and replaces, several forms which are separate in a Chapter 7 bankruptcy. This form asks a series of questions, and explains what information is requested. You should be able to complete the form simply by reading the form and answering the questions it asks.

For many of the questions there are two columns for the answers, one for the debtor and one for the debtor's spouse. If you are single, simply type "N/A" in the column for the spouse. If you are married, be sure you answer each question for both yourself and your spouse. Although most of the questions are self-explanatory, some clarification of the following items may help:

Item 2f(6). The most common wage assignment is one which deducts child support payments directly from your paycheck.

Item 4b. Although this asks for the "family" expenses, it is separated between you and your spouse. All that Item 4 is really asking for is your total income minus your total expenses. This will show how much money you have left over to pay your creditors under your payment plan (which you will prepare later).

Item 5. As you are preparing these papers yourself, you will probably be answering these questions with "N/A". If you are represented by an attorney, he or she should be completing these forms for you. If you have consulted and paid a lawyer for some advice, but he is not handling the bankruptcy for you, fill in how much you have paid him and add the following statement: "For advice provided, but attorney was not retained."

Item 12a. Most of the questions under this part relate to operation of a business. If you operated a business you should consult a lawyer. Otherwise, the only item which you may need to be concerned with is 12a, Column (1), item "f," relating to taxes you owe. Be sure to total the appropriate Columns where indicated, and complete the Unsworn Declaration Under Penalty of Perjury at the bottom of this form.

E. CHAPTER 13 PLAN (FORM 13).

The CHAPTER 13 PLAN is your explanation of how and what you intend to pay your creditors from your disposable income. At the top of the third page of your CHAPTER 13 STATEMENT (FORM 12), which you just prepared, in item 4c, is your disposable income. This is the amount of money you have available to turn over to the trustee in order to pay your debts. The following instructions will help you complete your CHAPTER 13 PLAN.

First, complete the top portion of the form. The figure in item 4c of FORM 12 is a monthly figure. If you receive a paycheck monthly you can use this figure. However, if you are paid on a weekly or semi-monthly basis, you will need to convert this figure. If you are paid weekly, divide the monthly figure by 4.3. If you are paid every two weeks, multiply the monthly figure by 12, then divide by 26. If you are paid twice a month, divide the monthly figure by 2. Your answer will go on the line in the first paragraph of your CHAPTER 13 PLAN. You will then cross out the pay periods which do not apply to you. For example, if you are paid on a semi-monthly basis, you would cross out the words "(weekly)" and "(monthly)."

Next, you will complete paragraph 2 by describing how you want to pay your secured debts. Remember, if you don't pay secured debts the lender can repossess the property. Therefore, you will want to keep up the payments on these debts. List the name of the lender, the amount of the debt, and the monthly payment to be made.

Now complete paragraph 3 by describing how you want to pay your unsecured debts. First, deduct the total amount of your payments on your secured debts from your disposable income. This will give you how much you have left to pay your unsecured creditors. Generally, you must pay each unsecured creditor the same percentage of the debt over a three year period. If you have enough income to pay all of these debts in full within three years, you will set up a schedule to accomplish this.

To determine how much of your debts you can pay, use the following steps:
1. Take your monthly disposable income (from item 4c of FORM 12), subtract the total monthly payments to secured creditors, and multiply the answer by 36. This will give you the total amount you have available to pay over three years.
2. Add up the total amount you owe to all of your unsecured creditors.
3. Divide the total from "2" above by the total amount in "1." This will give you the percentage of each debt you will be able to pay.
4. For each debt, multiply the total amount owed by the percentage from "3."
5. Take the answer from "4" and divide it by 36. This will give you how much of your monthly disposable income should be applied to each debt. Convert this to match your pay period if necessary (such as to a weekly or semi-monthly amount).

In paragraph 3 of FORM 13, type in the name of the creditor, the amount to be paid each month, and the percentage of the amount due that will be paid.

Paragraph 5 of FORM 13 contains a box to be checked if there is an addendum to the form. This will be used if you need additional space to complete this form, or if there are any particular arrangements regarding the payment of your debts.

Finally, date and sign the form. This form should be filed along with your petition, and must be filed no more than 15 days after you file your petition.

SECTION 13. FILING WITH THE CLERK, ETC.

Once all of your papers have been prepared, you are ready to file them with the court clerk. This is not difficult, however, things will go smoother if you are organized and know what you can expect.

A. FINDING THE CLERK'S OFFICE.

By now you should have found out where the bankruptcy court is located. If not, the first place to check is the government listings in your local telephone directory. Look in the U.S. Government section for "Bankruptcy Court," "District Court" or "Clerk of the District Court." If this fails, there is probably a general U.S. government "information" listing. Call the number and ask where the bankruptcy court clerk's office is located. Also ask for directions, if you need them, and ask for the mailing address.

Only a few cities in each state have a federal court, so you may need to do some digging to find the closest one to you. If you are having trouble, try calling the law library at the county courthouse in your county, or try your local public library.

B. BANKRUPTCY PETITION COVER SHEET. (FORM 14).

Most, if not all, bankruptcy courts require you to complete a cover sheet to be filed with your petition. Check with your court clerk to see if they have their own form, otherwise use FORM 14 in APPENDIX A of this book. This is used by the clerk for a quick reference to the type of bankruptcy you are filing, and for statistical purposes. Simply read each box on the form and fill in the information required. The clerk will fill in case number. The "Type of Petition" is "Voluntary Petition." The "Nature of Debt" is "Non-business/Consumer."

Under the section for "Debtor's Estimates," use the information in the papers you have prepared. This section also asks if you expect any assets to be available for your creditors. If the only non-exempt property left will be items of clothing, old furniture, etc., check the box for "No assets will be available for distrubution to creditors." The trustee will most likely abandon old items of little value, even such things as 10 to 15 year old vehicles with a value of $300. It simply isn't worth the effort to try to sell the items. Remember, these are only estimates.

C. THE MAILING MATRIX. (FORM 15).

This is used by the clerk to make mailing labels in order to send notices to your creditors, and to you. Place a blank sheet of paper over the mailing matrix, and type in the following addresses, being careful to keep each one within a box: Type your name and address in the top left-hand box, then type in all of your creditors names and addresses in alphabetical order in the other box, moving across the page from left to right. Check with the court clerk to find out if they have their own mailing matrix form, or any special requirements as to how they want it completed. Be sure to follow the clerk's instructions carefully. Also,

-Include anyone who co-signed a loan.
-Include anyone jointly liable for a debt.
-Include your ex-spouse if you intend to discharge debts you assumed in the divorce.
-Include all creditors listed in the forms you just completed.
-Do not include your spouse if you are filing jointly.

D. WHAT TO BRING.

If you are filing for a Chapter 7 bankruptcy, you should bring:

-Bankruptcy Petition Cover Sheet (FORM 14).
-Voluntary Petition (FORM 4).
-Schedules A & B (FORM 7).
-Schedule of Current Income and Current Expenditures (FORM 8).
-Statement of Financial Affairs for Debtor Not Engaged in Business (FORM 9).
-Individual Debtor's Statement of Intention (FORM 10).
-Statement of Executory Contracts (FORM 11).
-Mailing Matrix (FORM 15).
-Check or money order for the filing fee.
-Note pad or paper, and pen, for writing down any information or instructions the court clerk may give you.

If you are filing for a Chapter 13 bankruptcy, you need to bring:

-Bankruptcy Petition Cover Sheet (FORM 14).
-Voluntary Petition (FORM 5).
-Statement of Financial Affairs for Debtor Not Engaged in Business (FORM 9).
-Chapter 13 Statement (FORM 12).
-Mailing Matrix (FORM 15).
-Check or money order for the filing fee.
-Note pad or paper, and pen, for writing down any information or instructions the court clerk may give you.

Under either Chapter 7 or Chapter 13, you may also be filing an Application to Pay Filing Fee in Installments (FORM 6), which needs to be filed with your other documents. If you are filing this document, your check or money order should be for the amount of the first payment listed on FORM 6. For either type of bankruptcy, be sure you have at least the number of copies required by the clerk, plus a copy for yourself.

E. FILING.

Although it is possible to file by mail, it is strongly advised that you actually go to the clerk's office and file in person. It is easier to establish a friendly relationship in person, and the more time you spend at the bankruptcy court the more comfortable you will feel with the entire process.

As you enter the clerk's office, look around for any signs that may help you figure out exactly where to go. There may be several "windows," which may be marked for different purposes, such as "Filing," "Cashier," "File Check-out," etc. Go to the appropriate window, or to any window if you are uncertain, and tell the clerk, "I'd like to file a Chapter 7" or "I'd like to file a Chapter 13."

The clerk will take your papers and examine them (or refer you to the proper window, where that clerk will take them). If everything looks in order, the clerk will then tell you how to go about paying the filing fee. Either that clerk will handle the payment, or you will be directed to the cashier's window. You will pay the filing fee, and receive a receipt. The clerk will also assign a case number, and will stamp or write the number on your papers. The case number should also be on your receipt. Your papers are now filed.

If the clerk determines that something is not correct with your papers, you will be told what is wrong. DO NOT ARGUE WITH THE CLERK. The clerk controls your access to the bankruptcy system, and you don't want to make an enemy of the clerk. Clerks cannot give you legal advice, but they will usually tell you what is wrong with your papers, and give you some idea of how you can fix the problem. The kind of problem the clerk will identify is one of form, such as you forgot to sign something, forgot to fill in a space, need another type of form, need to submit an extra copy, etc. All you can do is find out what the clerk wants, then do it. You may be able to correct the problem at the clerk's office.

If you try to satisfy the clerk, but are still getting your papers rejected or don't understand what is required, you may want to consult a lawyer. You can also politely tell the clerk that you aren't understanding the problem, and ask him or her to explain it again, or have another clerk try to explain it to you. Although most clerks are pleasant, helpful people, you sometimes run into a simply nasty clerk. You must still be polite, and try to win over the clerk; but if this doesn't work there is nothing wrong with asking for the clerk's supervisor. Just don't get angry under any circumstances. Remain calm and polite.

F. STOP MAKING PAYMENTS.

If you haven't already stopped making payments, you should stop once your petition is filed. From this point on, all payments for anything must be approved by the trustee. It's alright to buy food, gas for your car so you can get to work, and to pay for any necessary medical expenses, but that's about all. It will take awhile to have a trustee appointed, but as soon as you receive a notice in the mail with the name of the trustee, contact the trustee as soon as possible. Tell him that you just wanted to make an initial contact, and ask him if it is alright to pay any bills you feel you need to pay. Also ask him any other questions you have. If you are continuing to make payments on secured property (such as your mortgage or car payment), mention this to the trustee.

Filing your petition operates as an "automatic stay," which prohibits your creditors from taking any collection action, or from cutting off any services to you. Once your petition is filed, you may want to be sure to get your creditors off your back by sending them a letter notifying them that you have filed. FORM 16, found in AP-PENDIX a of this book, is a form letter for this purpose. Space is left at the top for the date and the creditor's address. Sign your name at the bottom, and below your name, type in your name, address and account number. If you have a particularly bothersome creditor, you may want to send the letter by certified, return-receipt mail. Let the trustee know if any creditors continue to bother you.

SECTION 14. CREDITORS MEETING

After you have filed your case, the clerk will do several things. Using the mailing matrix you provided and the information in your supporting documents, the clerk will send a notice to all of your creditors telling them that you have filed for bankruptcy. A trustee will also be appointed to your case, who will then schedule a meeting of creditors. Copies of any documents issued by the clerk or the trustee will be sent to you. Read them carefully, and call the clerk's office if you don't understand them. Most of these papers will not require you to do anything, but some may require some kind of a response.

You may also receive copies of any papers your creditors may file with the clerk. Again, these don't require you to do anything, but keep copies anyway.

You will receive a notice of the date, time and place of the meeting of creditors, which you must attend. The nature of this meeting varies slightly depending upon whether you selected a Chapter 7 or a Chapter 13 proceeding.

A. CHAPTER 7 CASES.

In a large number of cases no creditors come to the meeting. The trustee will review your papers and ask you some questions. The questions are usually to verify what is in your papers, or to fill in information which you may have left out.

A few days before the meeting, call the trustee and ask him to tell you what information you should bring to the creditors meeting. In all cases, be sure to bring copies of all the papers you filed and all the papers you have received regarding your case. You should also bring tax returns and other documents which support the information in the papers you filed. Each court may have its own particular requirements, which is why it is a good idea to ask the trustee.

If creditors do attend the meeting, they also have the right to ask you questions. A creditor's usual concern is whether you have identified all of your non-exempt property, and whether such property has been turned over to the trustee for sale. Answer all of the questions honestly, as you will be under oath.

If the trustee decides that your non-exempt property is not worth enough to justify trying to sell it, he may "abandon" the property. This means that you will get to keep it, even though it is not exempt.

B. CHAPTER 13 CASES.

Creditors are more likely to attend the meeting in a Chapter 13 case than in a Chapter 7 case. They are concerned about getting the most possible out of your proposed payment plan. They will ask questions about the reasonableness of your payment plan, and the likelihood that you will be able to carry it out. The trustee will also ask some questions. Again, you are under oath, so answer honestly.

If the creditors and the trustee approve of your plan, it will be accepted by the court. If the plan is not approved, you may either negotiate changes in the plan to make it acceptable, stick to your plan and let the judge decide if it is acceptable, or convert your case to a Chapter 7 bankruptcy. To convert your case, see Section 16 of this book, entitled "SPECIAL CIRCUMSTANCES."

Once your plan is approved, the trustee will probably order that the payments be deducted directly from your paycheck by your employer. This amount will be sent to the trustee, who will make the required payments to the individual creditors. Until the paycheck deduction goes into effect, however, you are responsible for making certain that the payments are made. Unless the court orders something different, payments must begin 30 days after you file your plan with the court. This may be before the creditors meeting, in which case you should still begin your payments. If your plan ends up not being approved, the creditors will be required to refund any payments you have made.

SECTION 15. THE COURT HEARING AND DISCHARGE

Depending upon the procedures in your particular bankruptcy court, you may or may not have to appear before the judge. If the trustee determines that everything is in order, you may receive a discharge without having to attend a hearing. In a Chapter 7 bankruptcy, once you have done all that is required to settle the case (turned over your non-exempt assets to the trustee, paid all the filing fee and any other costs required, etc.) an order will be entered discharging all of your dischargeable debts. As has already been discussed, you will not be discharged from the following types of debts:

-Taxes, fines or penalties owed to the government.
-Alimony or child support.
-Certain types of student loans.
-Obligations as a result of criminal or fraudulent actions.
-Any debts which were not declared in your bankruptcy, or which involve creditors not timely notified.

In a Chapter 13 case, you will be entitled to a discharge once you have completed all of the payments required by your payment plan. This is more likely to require a brief court hearing with the judge.

In either case, the judge will probably only talk to you about the effects of the bankruptcy discharge, caution you to avoid getting in debt again, and possibly ask a few questions to assure himself that everything has been done properly, and that you understand the meaning of the discharge. Your particular bankruptcy court may even have mass discharge hearings, in which many debtors are discharged at the same time and no questions are asked. All the judge does is give everyone a brief lecture about how your debts are now discharged, and how you should avoid getting into financial trouble again.

SECTION 16. SPECIAL CIRCUMSTANCES

This SECTION will discuss several matters which do not apply to most simple bankruptcy cases. However, they are important to mention just in case they may apply to you. If any of these situations do apply to your case, you may want to discuss them with a lawyer. Of course you should take a look at how much you may save, in contrast to how much a lawyer may cost you. The first two items mentioned have forms in APPENDIX A of this book, and you can probably do them without an attorney. However, the other items will require an attorney's assistance.

A. AMENDING YOUR PAPERWORK.

If, after you file your petition and other papers, you discover that you have made an error, you may amend whatever papers are necessary to correct the error. This will involve completing the AMENDMENT COVER SHEET (FORM 21), as well as whatever form or forms you need to amend. Some courts will require you to fully complete the form, while others will allow you to simply note the item being changed. You will need to call the court clerk to find out which you need to do. At the same time, ask the clerk if there is any filing fee for the amended form.

To complete FORM 21, after the first sentence, type in the name of the form or forms you are amending. Be sure to also complete the top portion of the form, as well as the date and signature portions at the bottom. Then attach the amended forms containing the new or changed information. You need to be sure to check whether the new information on one form also requires new information on other forms, and to include all forms which need changing. Also, certain changes may mean that you need to re-notify creditors, especially if the creditors meeting has already been held. Check with the trustee or clerk to see if you need to re-notify all of your creditors. If you do, you will need to send a copy of your AMENDMENT COVER SHEET and the changed documents to each creditor, and will need to complete a CERTIFICATE OF MAILING (FORM 18). To complete FORM 18 fill in the title of the documents you send, and the name and address of all the creditors or others you send copies to. If the creditors' meeting has already been held, another meeting may need to be scheduled.

B. CHANGING FROM CHAPTER 13 TO CHAPTER 7.

If you filed your case under Chapter 13 of the bankruptcy act, and have determined that you need to convert your case to Chapter 7, you need to complete the FORM 22 in APPENDIX A or this book, entitled MOTION AND ORDER TO CONVERT TO CHAPTER 7. This form only requires you to complete the top portion and the date and signature portion. At the time you file this form, also include the other forms needed for a Chapter 7 bankruptcy as described in SECTION 11 of this book.

C. LIEN AVOIDANCE.

This is a procedure which allows a debtor to keep certain property which might otherwise be subject to repossession. Before reading about this any further, you should know that this is not available if you live in the following states: Kentucky, Louisiana, Maryland, Mississippi, Tennessee, and Utah. Also, it is only available if you use the federal exemptions in the following states: Alaska, Connecticut, Texas, and Washington. With the possible exception of Connecticut, it is most likely that you will find the state exemptions more of an advantage in these states, especially if you own a home. Furthermore, lien avoidance only applies to exempt property, and you can't avoid more than the exemption allows.

Next, you need to see if you have either of the two types of liens to which this can apply: (1) those created by a court judgment, and (2) those created when you used your existing property as security for a loan. You may not avoid a lien if you took out the loan in order to buy the secured piece of property. Therefore, if you have no court judgments, and your secured debts all relate to the item you purchased, you are not eligible for lien avoidance.

There are three other important limitations on the use of lien avoidance. First, you can't use this to avoid a lien on your vehicle, unless it is used as a part of your business (which does not include use to get to and from work). Second, if the lien is for more than the exemption amount for that item, the lien will only be reduced and the creditor may still repossess if the amount remaining isn't paid immediately. Third, lien avoidance can only be accomplished by filing more papers with the court, possibly leading to a court battle with the creditor, and even the necessity for an appraisal of the property.

D. REDEMPTION.

This is where you agree to pay the creditor a lump sum, based upon the market value of a piece of exempt property. This is generally only advisable if the property is worth less than the amount owed on the loan. Instead of paying off the full loan, you only pay the amount the property is worth. This is done because if the creditor repossesses the property, he will only be able to sell it for the market value as the remainder of the loan is discharged in the bankruptcy.

However, there are limitations here also. First, three conditions must be met: (1) the debt must be a consumer debt, meaning it is for personal use, as opposed to business use, (2) it must be for tangible, personal property (as opposed to items like stocks and bonds), and (3) you must be claiming the property as exempt, or the trustee must abandon the property (which is usually done because the property is of little value).

E. REAFFIRMING A DEBT.

This is where you and your creditor agree that the debt will still be owed after the bankruptcy and that you will continue to make payments. This requires a written agreement, signed by you and your creditor, and must contain certain provisions. A preferable alternative to this is for you to bring your payments current before filing for bankruptcy, and keep up your payments so the loan is not in default. Reaffirmation should be a last resort, as it takes negotiating with the creditor, leaves you still liable for a debt, and requires the preparation of a written legal agreement. Economically, reaffirmation often only makes sense if the loan is not current, you owe considerably less money than the property is worth, and the property is exempt.

F. LAWSUITS.

If you are involved in a lawsuit in which anyone is suing for money (such as a personal injury lawsuit), seeking to collect a debt, or to foreclose or repossess your property, you need to immediately notify the court and the creditor that you have filed for bankruptcy. This will bring the lawsuit to a dead stop, and your creditor will have to get the bankruptcy court judge's permission before he can continue with the lawsuit. The formal way to do this is to file a SUGGESTION OF BANKRUPTCY (FORM 17 in APPENDIX A or this book) with the court where the lawsuit is pending. DO NOT file this in the bankruptcy court. You will need to complete the top portion of the form in exactly the same manner as your other court papers in the lawsuit read, and file it with the clerk of that court (NOT the bankruptcy clerk).

SECTION 17. THE AFTERMATH

Once you receive your discharge, you need to think about the future. The two main things you need to do are make sure that you don't get into financial trouble again, and start building credit again.

A. HANDLING YOUR FINANCES.

By preparing FORM 1 you should have an idea of how do prepare a budget. FORM 20 is a budget form. Make additional copies of it to use in the months ahead. Your budgeting has three main goals:

1. Assuring that you aren't spending more than you earn.
2. Assuring that you will have the money available when the bill is due.
3. Developing a savings plan.

First of all, you should have a checking account if you don't already. Shop around for a bank with the lowest minimum balance for free checking, or the lowest checking charges. There are dozens of different checking account arrangements, so compare. Use the top line of the first column in FORM 20 to write in the total amount in your checking account. Your job is to decide which of the debts listed needs to be paid before your next paycheck, and how much of the total needs to be assigned to each of those debts. Use the other columns to allocate your next several paychecks to your debts. Hopefully, after you deduct all of the debt payments from the amounts in the top column, you will have something left over.

Ideally, experts say, you should save approximately 10% of each paycheck. For many people this seems impossible. But that is no excuse for not trying to save something. If you have never saved, try it for awhile. You may be surprised to find out that the feeling you get from looking at a bank account balance with an emergency cushion of $200 or $1,000 is as good as the feeling you'd get from spending that money.

The important thing is not to buy something unless you know exactly where you will get the money to pay for it when the bill is due. Whenever you think about buying on credit, look at your budget and ask yourself where the money will come from. It certainly can't come from the rent money, or from the food money... It should only come from the "Spending" money, such as from next week's paycheck. If so, then subtract that amount from the "Spending" line in the column for next week's check, and write it on one of the lines for "Credit Payments," also writing in the name of the store or other credit card involved.

B. OBTAINING CREDIT. (IF YOU DARE!)

One of the problems, or maybe it's a blessing in disguise, of going through a bankruptcy is that it will be difficult to obtain credit. During the bankruptcy you "enjoyed" finding out what life is like without the use of credit, and it's a good idea to do without credit until you are sure that you can keep your finances under control. However, in our society, credit is almost essential if one is to improve one's standard of living.

Generally, buying a home is a better deal than renting one. Also, some essential items, such as cars, are very difficult to pay cash for. So it is a good idea to begin establishing some credit once you have things under control.

One way to begin is to apply for a credit card from a local store. Almost every type of store now has its own credit cards, particularly local department stores and hardware stores. Many of these stores will issue a temporary card immediately upon filling out an application. Go into the store, fill out the application (which usually only asks your name, address and where you work), then buy something immediately with the temporary card. Even if the application is later rejected, you still have an obligation to make the payments on the item you bought, and that repayment will be something positive in your new credit record. You can always do the same thing the next time you need to buy something at that store. Eventually, your timely payment will be noticed and you will get an application for a permanent card approved.

Until you get a few local cards, and establish a payment record on each, you should avoid applying for a major card (such as VISA or Mastercard), and avoid applying for a card at a major, nationwide department store (such as Sears or J.C Penney). Such applications will almost certainly be rejected.

Another way to establish credit is to borrow against your own money. If you can accumulate some money in a savings account, the bank will probably allow you to borrow money with the savings account as collateral. Once you pay back the money you borrowed, you've taken the first step toward establishing a positive credit history. You will have to pay a little interest, but the object here is to establish credit, not make a brilliant deal. For example, say you have $500 in a savings account. Borrow $250 against the account for a period of 30 days. Take the $250 and put it in your checking account. At the end of the 30 days, write a check to pay off the loan (at an annual interest rate of 15%, this will mean writing a check for about $253.13). You will be paying $3.13 interest for the privilege of establishing some credit, which is not very expensive.

APPENDIX A

FORMS

This APPENDIX contains the forms referred to in the various Sections of this book. Make several copies of these forms to use, and save the originals in case you make mistakes or wish to make changes later.

Be sure to check with the court clerk before you begin using these forms. Your particular court may require you to use special forms, in which case they will not accept the forms from this book. If your court requires you to use certain forms, then use them. The court may provide the forms, or you may need to buy them. If this is the case, ask the clerk to tell you where you may purchase the forms. Whatever forms your court requires, they will require the same information as the forms in this book (and probably in the same order, with exactly the same wording), so you can still follow the instructions in this book for filling out the forms.

TABLE OF FORMS

INCOME AND EXPENSE STATEMENT

INCOME (Monthly):
    Take Home Pay (wages, salary, commissions)   _____
    Self Employment Income   _____
    Interest and Dividends   _____
    Income From Real Estate   _____
    Retirement Income   _____
    Alimony or Support Payments   _____
    Other:_____   _____
    _____   _____

TOTAL MONTHLY INCOME   _____

EXPENSES (Monthly):
    Mortgage or Rent   _____
    Homeowners/Renters Insurance   _____
    Real Estate Taxes   _____
    Electricity   _____
    Gas   _____
    Water   _____
    Telephone   _____
    Garbage Pick-up   _____
    Other:_____   _____
    Home Repair/Maintenance   _____
    Auto Loan   _____
    Other Installment Loan Payments:

    _____   _____
    _____   _____
    _____   _____
    _____   _____
    _____   _____

    Auto Insurance   _____
    Gasoline   _____
    Auto Repairs/Maintenance   _____
    Food   _____
    Clothing   _____
    Medical, Dental, and Medicines   _____
    Life Insurance   _____
    Laundry   _____
    Recreation/Travel/Entertainment   _____
    Education   _____
    License Fees, Dues, Memberships   _____
    Other Taxes   _____
    Other:_____   _____

    _____   _____
    _____   _____
    _____   _____
    _____   _____

TOTAL MONTHLY EXPENSES   _____

DEFICIT (Total Income - Total Expenses)   _____

PROPERTY INVENTORY

(1)PROPERTY	(2)VALUE	(3)AMT. OWED	(4)EQUITY	(5)EXEMPT	(6)SECURED
Real Estate:					
Autos, etc.:					
Boats, etc.:					
Cash on hand:					
Bank accts:					
Clothing:					
Jewelry:					
Household Goods:					
Collections:					
Sports Equip:					
Trade tools:					
Investments:					
Insurance:					
Other prop:					
TOTALS:					

DEBT INVENTORY

	(1)LENDER	(2)ITEM	(3)BALANCE	(4)SECURED	(5)DISCHARGEABLE
Real Estate:					
Autos, etc.:					
Boats, etc.:					
Credit Cards:					
Student Loans:					
Taxes Owed:					
Other Debts:					
TOTALS:					

UNITED STATES BANKRUPTCY COURT
_____ DISTRICT OF _____

In re _____   )
_____,   )
Debtor(s).   )   Case No._____
)
Social Security No(s).:   )
)
_____   )

VOLUNTARY PETITION – CHAPTER 7

    1.   Petitioner's mailing address, including county, is
_____.

    2.   Petitioner has resided within this district for the preceding 180 days, or for a longer portion of the preceding 180 days than in any other district.

    3.   Petitioner is qualified to file this petition and is entitled to the benefits of Title 11, United States Code, as a voluntary debtor.

    4.   Petitioner is aware that petitioner may proceed under Chapter 7, 11, 12 or 13 of Title 11, United States Code, understands the relief available under each such chapter, and chooses to proceed under Chapter 7 of such title.

    WHEREFORE, petitioner requests relief in accordance with Chapter 7 of Title 11, United States Code.

    The Petitioner(s) named in the foregoing petition, declare under penalty of perjury that the foregoing is true and correct.

Dated: _____

                Signed: _____
                         Petitioner

                        _____
                         Petitioner

UNITED STATES BANKRUPTCY COURT
_____ DISTRICT OF _____

In re _____   )
_____,)
Debtor(s).   )   Case No._____
)
Social Security No(s).:   )
_____   )

VOLUNTARY PETITION - CHAPTER 13

     1.   Petitioner's mailing address, including county, is
_____.

     2.   Petitioner has resided within this district for the preceding 180 days, or for a longer portion of the preceding 180 days than in any other district.

     3.   Petitioner is qualified to file this petition and is entitled to the benefits of Title 11, United States Code, as a voluntary debtor.

     4. A copy of petitioner's proposed plan, dated _____, is attached pursuant to Chapter 13 of Title 11, United States Code.

     5.   Petitioner is aware that petitioner may proceed under chapter 7, 11, 12 or 13 of Title 11, United States Code, understands the relief available under each such chapter, and chooses to proceed under Chapter 13 of such title.

     WHEREFORE, petitioner requests relief in accordance with Chapter 13 of Title 11, United States Code.

     The Petitioner(s) named in the foregoing petition, declare under penalty of perjury that the foregoing is true and correct.

Dated: _____

                Signed: _____
                               Petitioner

                              _____
                               Petitioner

UNITED STATES BANKRUPTCY COURT
_____ DISTRICT OF _____

In re _____   )
_____,   )
Debtor(s).   )   Case No._____
)
Social Security No(s):   )
_____   )

APPLICATION TO PAY FILING FEE IN INSTALLMENTS

In accordance with Bankruptcy Rule 1006, application is made for permission to pay the filing fee as follows:

$_____ upon filing of the petition, and balance of

$_____ in _____ installments, as follows:
$_____ on or before _____
$_____ on or before _____
$_____ on or before _____

I certify that I have not paid any money or transferred any property to an attorney or any other person for services in connection with this case or in connection with any other pending bankruptcy case and that I will not make any payment or transfer any property for services in connection with the case until the filing fee is paid in full.

Dated:_____   _____
                                                Applicant

                                     _____
                                                Applicant

                                     Address:_____

                                             _____

ORDER

IT IS ORDERED that the debtor pay the filing fee in installments on the terms set forth above.
IT IS FURTHER ORDERED that until the filing fee is paid in full the debtor shall not pay, and no person shall accept, any money for services in connection with this case, and the debtor shall not relinquish, and no person shall accept, any property as payment for services in connection with this case.

DATED:_____

                                     _____
                                              Bankruptcy Judge

UNITED STATES BANKRUPTCY COURT
_____ DISTRICT OF _____

In re _____)
_____ ,)
Debtor(s). _____) Case No._____
)
Social Security No(s): _____)
)
_____)

SCHEDULES A&B: LIABILITIES AND PROPERTY OF DEBTOR

SCHEDULE A: STATEMENT OF ALL LIABILITIES OF DEBTOR
Schedules A-1, A-2 and A-3 must include all claims against the debtor or debtor's property as of the date of filing the petition by the debtor.

Schedule A-1: Creditors Having Priority

(1) Nature of claim.	(2) Name of creditor and complete mailing address including zip code.	(3) Specify when claim was incurred and the consideration therefor; when claim is subject to setoff, evidenced by a judgment, negotiable instrument, or other writing, or incurred as partner or joint contractor, so indicate; specify name of any partner or joint contractor on any debt.	(4) Indicate if claim is contingent, unliquidated, or disputed.	(5) Amount of claim.
a. Wages, salary, and commissions, including vacation, severance and sick leave pay owing to employees not exceeding $2,000 to each, earned within 90 days before filing of petition or cessation of business (if earlier specify date).				
b. Contributions to employee benefit plans for services rendered within 180 before filing of petition or cessation of business (if earlier specify date).				
c. Claims of farmers, not exceeding $2,000 for each individual, pursuant to 11 U.S.C. Section 507(a)(5)(A).				
d. Claims of United States fishermen, not exceeding $2,000 for each individual, pursuant to 11 U.S.C. Section 507(a)(5)(B).				
e. Deposits by individuals, not exceeding $900 for each purchase, lease, or rental of property or services for personal, family, or household use that were not delivered or provided.				
f. Taxes owing (itemize by type of tax and taxing authority) (1) To the United States. (2) To any state. (3) To any other taxing authority				
TOTAL				

Schedule A-2: Creditors Holding Security

(1) Name of creditor and complete mailing address including zip code.	(2) Description of security and date when obtained by creditor.	(3) Specify when claim was incurred and the consideration therefor; when claim is subject to setoff, evidenced by a judgment, negotiable instrument, or other writing, or incurred as partner or joint contractor, so indicate; specify name of any partner or joint contractor on any debt.	(4) Indicate if claim is contingent, unliquidated, or disputed.	(5) Market Value.	(6) Amount of claim without deduction of value of security.
TOTAL					

81

Schedule A-3: Creditors Having Unsecured Claims Without Priority

(1) Name of creditor (including last known holder of any negotiable instrument) and complete mailing address including zip code.	(2) Specify when claim was incurred and the consideration therefor; when claim is contingent, unliquidated, disputed, subject to setoff, evidenced by a judgment, negotiable instrument, or other writing, or incurred as partner or joint contractor, so indicate; specify name or any partner or joint contractor on any debt.	(3) Indicate if claim is contingent, unliquidated, or disputed.	(4) Amount of claim.
TOTAL			

SCHEDULE B: STATEMENT OF ALL PROPERTY OF DEBTOR

Schedules B-1, B-2, B-3 and B-4 must include all property of the debtor as of the date of filing the petition.

Schedule B-1: Real Property

(1) Description and location of all real property in which debtor has an interest (including equitable and future interests, interests in estates by the entirety, community property, life estates, leaseholds, and rights and powers exercisable for the debtor's own benefit).	(2) Nature of interest (specify all deeds and written instruments relating thereto).	(3) Market value of debtor's interest without deduction for secured claims listed in Schedule A-2 or exemptions claimed in Schedule B-4.
TOTAL		

Schedule B-2: Personal Property

(1) Type of Property	(2) Description and Location.	(3) Market value of debtor's interest without deduction for secured claims listed on Schedule A-2 or exemptions claimed on Schedule B-4.
a. Cash on hand.		
b. Deposits of money with banking institutions, savings and loan associations, brokerage houses, credit unions, public utility companies, landlords and others.		
c. Household goods, supplies and furnishings.		
d. Books, pictures, and other art objects; stamp, coin, and other collections.		
e. Wearing apparel, jewelry, firearms, sports equipment and other personal possessions.		
f. Automobiles, trucks, trailers and other vehicles.		

(1) Type of Property	(2) Description and Location.	(3) Market value of debtor's interest without deduction for secured claims listed on Schedule A-2 or exemptions claimed on Schedule B-4.
g. Boats, motors and their accessories.		
h. Livestock, poultry and other animals.		
i. Farming equipment, supplies and implements.		
j. Office equipment, furnishings and supplies.		
k. Machinery, fixtures, equipment and supplies (other than those listed in Items j and l) used in business.		
l. Inventory.		
m. Tangible personal property of any other description.		
n. Patents, copyrights, licenses, franchises and other general intangibles (specify all documents and writings relating thereto).		
o. Government and corporate bonds and other negotiable and nonnegotiable instruments.		
p. Other liquidated debts owing debtor.		

(1) Type of Property	(2) Description and Location.	(3) Market value of debtor's interest without deduction for secured claims listed on Schedule A-2 or exemptions claimed on Schedule B-4.
q. Contingent and unliquidated claims of every nature, including counterclaims of the debtor (give estimated value of each).		
r. Interests in insurance policies (name insurance company of each policy and itemize surrender or refund value of each).		
s. Annuities (itemize and name each issuer).		
t. Stock and interests in incorporated and unincorporated companies (itemize separately).		
u. Interests in partnerships.		
v. Equitable and future interests, life estates, and rights or powers exercisable for the benefit of the debtor (other than those listed in Schedule B-1)(specify all written instruments relating thereto).		
TOTAL		

Schedule B-3: Property Not Otherwise Scheduled

(1) Type of Property.	(2) Description and Location.	(3) Market value of debtor's interest without deduction for secured claims listed in Schedule A-2 or exemption claimed in Schedule B-4.
a. Property transferred under assignment for benefit of creditors, within 120 days prior to filing of petition (specify date of assignment, name and address of assignee, amount realized there-from by the assignee, and disposition of proceeds so far known to debtor).		
b. Property of any kind not otherwise scheduled.		
TOTAL		

Schedule B-4: Property Claimed as Exempt

Debtor selects the following property as exempt pursuant to
___ 11 U.S.C Section 522(d)
___ the laws of the State of _____ .

(1) Type of Property.	(2) Location, description, and, so far as relevant to the claim of exemption, present use of property.	(3) Specify statute creating the exemption.	(4) Value claimed exempt.
TOTAL			

SUMMARY OF DEBTS AND PROPERTY

Debts

A-1/a,b.	Wages, etc., having priority	$_____
A-1/c,d	Claims of farmers, fishermen	_____
A-1/e	Deposits of money	_____
A-1/f(1)	Taxes owing United States	_____
A-1/f(2)	Taxes owing states	_____
A-1/f(3)	Taxes owing other taxing authorities	_____
A-2	Secured claims	_____
A-3	Unsecured claims without priority	_____
	Schedule A Total	$_____

Property

B-1	Real property (total value)	$_____
B-2/a	Cash on hand	_____
B-2/b	Deposits	_____
B-2/c	Household goods	_____
B-2/d	Books, pictures and collections	_____
B-2/e	Wearing apparel, personal possessions	_____
B-2/f	Automobiles and other vehicles	_____
B-2/g	Boats, motors and accessories	_____
B-2/h	Livestock and other animals	_____
B-2/i	Farming equipment and supplies	_____
B-2/j	Office equipment and supplies	_____
B-2/k	Machinery, equipment and supplies used in business	_____
B-2/l	Inventory	_____
B-2/m	Other tangible personal property	_____
B-2/n	Patents and other intangibles	_____
B-2/o	Bonds and other instruments	_____
B-2/p	Other liquidated debts	_____
B-2/q	Contingent and unliquidated claims	_____
B-2/r	Interests in insurance policies	_____
B-2/s	Annuities	_____
B-2/t	Interests in corporations and unincorporated companies	_____
B-2/u	Interests in partnerships	_____
B-2/v	Equitable and future interests, rights and powers in personal property	_____
B-3/a	Property assigned for benefit of creditors	_____
B-3/b	Property not otherwise scheduled	_____
	Schedule B Total	$_____

UNSWORN DECLARATION UNDER PENALTY OF PERJURY

I, _____ and I. _____, declare under penalty of perjury that I have read the foregoing schedules, consisting of _____ sheets, and that they are true and correct to the best of my knowledge, information and belief.

Executed on _____, 19___.

_____
Petitioner

_____
Petitioner

UNITED STATES BANKRUPTCY COURT
_____ DISTRICT OF _____

In re _____)
_____,)
Debtor(s).) Case No._____
)
Social Security No(s):)
_____)

SCHEDULE OF CURRENT INCOME AND EXPENDITURES
FOR INDIVIDUAL DEBTOR

A. Family Status.
  1. The debtor is (check one of the following): ___Married ___Single ___Separated ___Divorced
  2. The name of the debtor's spouse is _____
  3. The debtor supports the following dependents (other than the debtor's spouse):

Name	Age	Relationship to Debtor

B. Employment and Occupation.
  1. The debtor is employed by (name of employer):_____as
(nature of position)_____.
  2. The debtor is self-employed as (nature of business or profession)_____at the
following principal place of business (address):_____.
  3. The debtor's spouse is employed by (name of employer)_____as
(nature of position)_____.
  4. The debtor's spouse is self-employed as (nature of business or profession)_____at the
following principal place of business (address): _____.

C. Current Income.
  Give estimated average current monthly income of debtor and spouse, consisting of:

	Debtor	Spouse
1. Gross pay (wages, salary, or commissions)	$_____	$_____
2. Take home pay (gross pay less all deductions)	_____	_____
3. Regular income available from the operation of a business or profession	_____	_____
4. Other income:		
Interest and dividends	_____	_____
From real estate or personal property	_____	_____
Social security	_____	_____
Pension or other retirement income	_____	_____
Other (specify) _____	_____	_____
_____	_____	_____
5. Alimony, maintenance, or support payments:		
Payable to the debtor for the debtor's use	_____	_____
Payable to the debtor for the support of another (attach additional sheet listing the name, age and relationship to the debtor or persons for whose benefit payments are made)	_____	_____
Total estimated current monthly income.	$_____	$_____

  If you anticipate receiving additional income on other than a monthly basis in the next six months (such as an income tax refund), attach additional sheets of paper and describe.
  If you anticipate a substantial change in your income in the immediate future, attach additional sheet of paper and describe.

D. Schedule of Current Expenditures.

Give estimated average current monthly expenditures of debtor and spouse, consisting of:

1. Home expenses:
   a. Rent or home loan payment
      (including any assessment or maintenance fee) $_____
   b. Real estate taxes   _____
   c. Utilities:
      Electricity $_____
      Gas   _____
      Water   _____
      Telephone   _____
      Other (specify)_____   _____
      Total utilities   _____
   d. Home maintenance (repairs and upkeep)   _____
      Total of all home expenses $_____

2. Other expenses:
   a. Taxes (not deducted from wages or included in home loan
      payment or included in real estate taxes) $_____
   b. Alimony, maintenance or support payments (attach additional
      sheet listing name, age, and relationship of beneficiaries   _____
   c. Insurance (not deducted from wages):
      Life $_____
      Health   _____
      Auto   _____
      Homeowner's or renter's   _____
      Other (specify) _____   _____
      Total insurance expenses $_____
   d. Installment payments:
      Auto   _____
      Other (specify):_____   _____
      _____   _____
      _____   _____
      _____   _____
   e. Transportation (not including auto payment   _____
   f. Education (including tuition and books)   _____
   g. Food   _____
   h. Clothing   _____
   i. Medical, dental and medicines   _____
   j. Laundry and cleaning   _____
   k. Newspapers, periodicals and books   _____
   l. Recreation, clubs and entertainment   _____
   m. Charitable contributions   _____
   n. Other expenses (specify): _____   _____
   _____   _____

Total estimated current monthly expenses $_____

   If you anticipate a substantial change in your expenses in the immediate future attach additional sheet of paper and describe.

UNSWORN DECLARATION UNDER PENALTY OF PERJURY

I, _____ and I, _____, declare under penalty of perjury that I have read the foregoing schedules, consisting of ____ sheets, and that they are true and correct to the best of my knowledge, information and belief.

Executed on _____, 19___.

_____
Petitioner

_____
Petitioner

UNITED STATES BANKRUPTCY COURT
DISTRICT OF _____

In re _____)
_____)
_____,)
Debtor(s).)   Case No._____
)
Social Security No(s).:)
_____)

STATEMENT OF FINANCIAL AFFAIRS FOR DEBTOR
NOT ENGAGED IN BUSINESS

Each question shall be answered or the failure to answer explained. If the answer is "none" or "not applicable" so state. If additional space is needed for the answer to any question, a separate sheet, properly identified and made a part hereof, should be used and attached.

The term "original petition", used in the following questions, shall mean the petition filed under Rule 1002 or 1004.

	Debtor.	Spouse.
1. Name and residence.		
a. What is your full name?		
b Have you used, or been known by, any other names within the six years immediately preceding the filing of the original petition? (If so, give particulars)		
c. Where do you now reside?		
d. Where else have you resided during the six years immediately preceding the filing of the original petition?		
2. Occupation and income.		
a. What is your occupation?		
b. Where are you now employed? (Give the name and address of your employer, or the address at which you carry on your trade or profession, and the length of time you have been so employed or engaged).		
c. Have you been in a partnership with anyone, or engaged in any business during the six years immediately preceding the filing of the original petition? (If so, give particulars, including names, dates and places).		

	Debtor.	Spouse.

d. What amount of income have you received from your trade or profession during each of the two calendar years immediately preceding the filing of the original petition?

3. Tax returns and refunds.

   a. Where did you file your federal, state and municipal income tax returns for the two years immediately preceding the filing of the original petition?

   b. What tax refunds (income and other) have you received during the year immediately preceding the filing of the original petition?

   c. To what tax refunds (income and other), if any, are you, or may you be, entitled? (Give particulars, including information as to any refund payable jointly to you and your spouse or any other person).

4. Financial accounts, certificates of deposit and safe deposit boxes.

   a. What accounts or certificates of deposit or shares in banks, savings and loan, thrift, building and loan and homestead associations, credit unions, brokerage houses, pension funds and the like have you maintained alone or together with any other person, and in your own or any other name within the two years immediately preceding the filing of the original petition? (Give the name and address of each institution, the name and number under which the account or certificate is maintained, and the name and address of every other person authorized to make withdrawals from such account).

   b. What safe deposit box or boxes or other depository or depositories have you kept or used for your cash, securi-ties, or other valuables within the two years immediately preceding the filing of the original petition? (Give the name and address of the bank or other depository, the name in which each box or other depository was kept, the name and address of every other person who had the right of access thereto, a brief description of the contents thereof, and, if the box has been surrendered, state when surrendered, or, if transferred,

	Debtor.	Spouse.

when transferred, and the name and address of the transferee).

5. Books and records.

  a. Have you kept books of account or records relating to your affairs within the two years immediately preceding the filing of the original petition?

  b. In whose possession are these books or records? (Give names and addresses).

  c. If any of these books or records are not available, explain.

  d. Have any books or account or records relating to your affairs been destroyed, lost, or otherwise disposed of within the two years immediately preceding the filing of the original petition? (If so, give particulars, including date of destruction, loss, or disposition, and reason therefor).

6. Property held for another.person.

  What property do you hold for any other person? (Give name and address of each person, and describe th property, or value thereof, and all writings relating thereto).

7. Property held by another.

  Is any other person holding anything of value in which you have an interest? (Give name and address, location and description of the property, and circumstances of the holding).

8. Prior bankruptcy.

  What cases under the Bankruptcy Act or title 11, United States Code have previously been brought by or against you? (State the location of the bankruptcy court, the nature and number of each case, the date when it was filed, and whether a discharge was granted or denied, the case was dismissed, or a composition, arrangement, of plan was confirmed).

9. Receiverships, general assignments, and other modes of liquidation.

  a. Was any of your property, at the time of the filing of the original petition,

in the hands of a receiver, trustee, or
other liquidating agent? (If so, give a brief
description of the property, the name and
address of the receiver, trustee, or other
agent, and, if the agent was appointed in
a court proceeding, the name and location
of the court, the title and number of the
case, and the nature thereof).

b. Have you made any assignment of
your property for the benefit of your
creditors, or any general settlement with
your creditors, within one year immediately preceding the filing of the original
petition? (If so, give dates, the name and
address of the assignee, and a brief
statement of the terms of assignment or
settlement).

10. Suits, executions and attachments.

a. Were you a party to any suit pending
at the time of the filing of the original
petition? (If so, give the name and
location of the court and the title and
nature of the proceeding).

b. Were you party to any suit termi-
nated within the year immediately
preceding the filing of the original
petition? (If so, give the name and
location of the court, the title and nature
of the proceeding, and the result).

c. Has any of your property been
attached, garnished, or seized under any
legal or equitable process within the year
immediately preceding the filing of the
original petition? (If so, describe the
property seized or person garnished, and
at whose suit)

11. (a) Payment of loans, installment
purchases and other debts.

What payments in whole or in part
have you made during the year immediately preceding the filing of the original
petition on any of the following: (1) loans;
(2) installment purchases of goods and
services; and (3) other debts? (Give the
names and addresses of the persons
receiving payment, the amounts of the
loans or other debts and the purchase
price of the goods and services, the dates
of the original transactions, the amounts
and dates of payments and, it any of the
payees are your relatives or insiders, the
relationship; if the debtor is a partnership

	Debtor.	Spouse.

and any of the payees is or was a partner or a relative of partner, state the relationship; if the debtor is a corporation and any of the payees is or was an officer, director or stockholder, or a relative of an officer, director or stockholder, state the relationship).

(b) Setoffs.

What debts have you owed to any creditor, including any bank, which were set off by that creditor against a debt or deposit owing by the creditor to you during the year immediately preceding the filing of the original petition? (Give the names and addresses of the persons setting off such debts, the dates of the setoffs, the amount of the debts owing by you and to you and, if any of the creditors are your relatives or insiders, the relationship).

12. Transfers of property.

a. Have you made any gifts, other than ordinary and usual presents to family members and charitable donations, during the year immediately preceding the filing of the original petition? (If so, give names and addresses of donees and dates, description and value of gifts).

b. Have you made any other transfer, absolute or for the purpose of security, or any other disposition, or real or personal property during the year immediatelypreceding the filing of the original petition? (Give a description of the property, the date of the transfer or disposition, to whom transferred or how disposed of, and, if the transferee is a relative or insider, the relationship, the consideration, if any, received therefor, and the disposition of such consideration).

13. Repossessions and returns.

Has any property been returned to, or repossessed by, the seller or by a secured party during the year immediately preceding the filing of the original petition? (If so, give particulars, including the name and address of the party getting the property and its description and value).

	Debtor.	Spouse.

14. Losses.

   a. Have you suffered any losses from fire, theft, or gambling during the year immediately preceding the filing of the original petition? (If so, give particulars, including dates, names, and places, and the amounts of money or value and general description of property lost).

   b. Was the loss covered in whole or part by insurance? (If so, give particulars).

15. Payments or transfers to attorneys and other person.

   a. Have you consulted an attorney during the year immediately preceding or since filing the original petition? (Give dates, name and address).

   b. Have you during the year immediately preceding or since the filing of the original petition paid any money or transferred any property to the attorney, to any other person on the attorney's behalf, or to any person rendering services to you in connection with this case? (If so, give particulars, including amount paid or value or property transferred and date of payment or transfer).

   c. Have you, either during the year immediately preceding or since the filing of the original petition, agreed to pay any money or transfer any property to an attorney at law, to any other person on the attorney's behalf, or to any other person rendering services to you in connection with this case? (If so, give particulars, including amount and terms of obligation).

UNSWORN DECLARATION UNDER PENALTY OF PERJURY

I, _____ and I, _____, declare under penalty of perjury that I have read the foregoing schedules, consisting of _____ sheets, and that they are true and correct to the best of my knowledge, information and belief.

Executed on _____ , 19___.

_____
Petitioner

_____
Petitioner

UNITED STATES BANKRUPTCY COURT
_____ DISTRICT OF _____

In re _____   )
)
_____,)   Case No. _____
Debtor(s).   )
)
Social Security No(s):   )
)
_____   )

CHAPTER 7 INDIVIDUAL DEBTOR'S STATEMENT OF INTENTION

1. I, _____, and I, _____, the debtor(s), have filed a schedule of assets and liabilities which includes consumer debts secured by property of the estate,

2. My intention with respect to the property of the estate which secures those consumer debts is as follows:

a. Property To Be Surrendered.

Description of Property	Creditor's Name

b. Property to Be Retained.

(1) Description of property.	(2) Creditor's name.	(3) The debt will be reaffirmed pursuant to Section 524(c).	(4) The property is claimed as exempt and will be redeemed pursuant to Section 722.	(5) The creditor's lien will be avoided pursuant to Section 522(f) and the property will be claimed as exempt.

3. I understand that Section 521(2)(B) of the Bankruptcy Code requires that I perform the above stated intention within 45 days of the filing of this statement with the court, or within any extension of the 45 day period which the court may grant.

Dated:_____, 19_____.

_____
Petitioner

_____
Petitioner

UNITED STATES BANKRUPTCY COURT
_____ DISTRICT OF _____

In re _____)
_____,)
Debtor(s).   )   Case No._____
)
Social Security No(s):   )
_____)

STATEMENT OF EXECUTORY CONTRACTS

The debtor has the following executory contracts:

UNSWORN DECLARATION UNDER PENALTY OF PERJURY

I, _____, and I, _____, declare under penalty of perjury that the foregoing is true and correct to the best of my knowledge, information and belief.

Executed on _____, 19___.

_____
Petitioner

_____
Petitioner

UNITED STATES BANKRUPTCY COURT
DISTRICT OF _____

In re _____)
_____,)
Debtor(s).   )   Case No._____
)
Social Security No(s).:   )
_____)

CHAPTER 13 STATEMENT

Each question shall be answered or the failure to answer explained. If the answer is "none" or "not applicable," so state. If additional space is needed for the answer to any question, a separate sheet, properly identified and made a part hereof, should be used and attached.

The term "original petition,", used in the following questions, shall mean the original petition filed under Section 301 of the Code or, if the chapter 13 case was converted from another chapter of the Code, shall mean the petition by or against you which originated the first case.

This form must be completed in full whether a single or a joint petition is filed. When information is requested for "each" or "either spouse filing a petition," it should be supplied for both when a joint petition is filed.

	Debtor.	Spouse.
1. Name and residence.		
a. Give full name.		
b. Where does debtor now reside? (Give mailing address, including zip code, and telephone number, including area code).		
c. What does debtor consider his or her residence, if different from that listed in b above?		
2. Occupation and income.		
a. Give present occupation. (If more than one, list all).		
b. What is the name, address and telephone number of present employer of debtor? (Also include any identifying badge or card number with employer).		
c. How long has debtor been employed by present employer?		
d. If debtor has not been employed by present employer for a period of one year, state the name of prior employer(s) and nature of employment during that period.		
e. Has debtor operated a business, in partnership or otherwise, during the past three years? (If so, give particulars, including names, dates and places).		

	Debtor.	Spouse.

f. Answer the following questions for debtor, if single, or each spouse whether single or joint petition is filed unless spouses are separated and a single petition is filed:

   (1) What are your gross wages, salary or commissions per pay period?

     (a) Weekly
     (b) Semi-monthly
     (c) Monthly
     (d) Other (specify)

   (2) What are your payroll deductions per pay period?

     (a) Payroll taxes (including Social Security)
     (b) Insurance
     (c) Credit union
     (d) Union dues
     (e) Other (specify)

   (3) What is your take-home pay per pay period?

   (4) What was the amount of your gross income for the last calendar year?

   (5) Is your employment subject to seasonal or other change?

   (6) Has either of you made any wage assignments or allotments? (If so, indicate which spouse's wages assigned or allotted, the name and address of the person to whom assigned or allotted, and the amount owing, if any, to such person. If allotment or assignment is to a creditor, the claim should also be listed in Item 11a.)

3. Dependents. (To be answered by debtor if unmarried, otherwise for each spouse whether single or joint petition is filed unless spouses are separated and a single petition is filed).

a. Does either of you pay (or receive) alimony, maintenance or support? (If so, indicate how much per month, and for whose support, giving the name, age and relationship to you).

	Debtor.	Spouse.

b. List all other dependents, other than present spouse, not listed in a above. (Give name, age and relationship to you).

4. Budget.

a. Give your estimated average future monthly income, if unmarried, otherwise for each spouse whether single or joint petition is filed, unless spouses are separated and a single petition is filed.

  (1) Monthly take-home pay
  (2) Other monthly income.
  TOTAL

b. Give estimated average future monthly expenses of family (not including debts to be paid under plan), consisting of:

  (1) Rent or home mortgage payment (include lot rental for trailer).
  (2) Utilities
    (a) Electricity
    (b) Heat
    (c) Water
    (d) Telephone
    (e) Other:_____
  (3) Food
  (4) Clothing
  (5) Laundry and cleaning
  (6) Newspapers, periodicals and books (including school books)
  (7) Medical and drug expenses
  (8) Insurance (not deducted from wages)
    (a) Auto
    (b) Other (specify)
  (9) Transportation (not including auto payments to be paid under plan).
  (10) Recreation
  (11) Dues, union, professional, social or otherwise (not deducted from wages)
  (12) Taxes (not deducted from wages
  (13) Alimony, maintenance or support payments
  (14) Other payments for support of dependents not living at home.

  (15) Religious and other charitable contributions
  (16) Other (specify)

    _____
    _____

TOTAL EXPENSES

	Debtor.	Spouse.

c. Excess of estimated future monthly income (last line of Item 4a above) over estimated future expenses (last line of Item 4b above).

d. Total amount to be paid each month under plan.

5.Payment of attorney.

a. How much have you agreed to pay or what property have you agreed to transfer to your attorney in connection with this case?

b. How much have you paid or what have you transferred to the attorney?

6. Tax refunds. (To be answered by debtor, if unmarried, otherwise for each spouse whether single or joint petition is filed, unless spouses are separated and a single petition is filed).

To what tax refunds (income or other), if any, is either of you, or may either of you be, entitled? (Give particulars, including information as to any refunds payable jointly to you or any other person. All such refunds should also be listed in Item 13b).

7. Financial accounts, certificates of deposit and safe deposit boxes. (To be answered by debtor, in unmarried, otherwise for each spouse whether single or joint petition is filed unless spouses are separated and a single petition is filed)

a. Does either of you currently have any accounts or certificates of deposit or shares in banks, savings and loan, thrift, building and loan, and homestead associations, credit unions, brokerage houses, pension funds and the like? (If so, give the name and address of each institution, number and nature of account, current balance, and name and address of every other person authorized to make withdrawals from the account. Such accounts should also be listed in Item 13b).

	Debtor.	Spouse.

b. Does either of you currently keep any safe deposit boxes or other depositories? (If so, give name and address of bank or other depository, name and address of every other person who has a right of access thereto, and a brief description of the contents thereof, which should also be listed in Item 13b).

8. Prior Bankruptcy.

What cases under the Bankruptcy Act or Bankruptcy Code have previously been brought by or against you or either spouse filing a petition? (State the location of the bankruptcy court, the nature and number of each case, the date when it was filed, and whether a discharge was granted or denied, the case was dismissed, or a composition, arrangement, or plan was confirmed).

9. Foreclosures, execution and attachments. (To be answered by debtor, if unmarried, otherwise for each spouse whether single or joint petition is filed unless spouses are separated and a single petition is filed).

a. Is any of the property of either of you, including real estate, involved in a foreclosure proceeding, in or out of court? (If so, identify the property and the person foreclosing).

b. Has any property or income of either of you been attached, garnished, or seized under any legal or equitable process within the 90 days immediately preceding the filing of the original petition? (If so, describe the property seized, or person garnished, and at whose suit).

	Debtor.	Spouse.

10. Repossessions and returns. (To be answered by debtor, if married, otherwise for each spouse whether single or joint petition is filed unless spouses are separated and a single petition is filed).

    Has any property of either of you been returned to, repossessed, or seized by the seller or by any other party, including a landlord, during the 90 days immediately preceding the filing of the original petition? (If so, give particulars, including the name and address of the party taking the property and its description and value).

11. Transfers of property. (To be answered by debtor, if married, otherwise for each spouse whether single or joint petition is filed unless spouses are separated and a single petition is filed).

a. Has either of you made any gifts, other than ordinary and usual presents to family members and charitable donations, during the year immediately preceding the filing of the original petition? (If so, give names and addresses of donees and dates, description and value of gifts).

b. Has either of you made any other transfer, absolute or for the purpose of security, or any other disposition, of real or personal property during the year immediately preceding the filing of the original petition? (If so, give a description of the property, the date of the transfer or disposition, to whom transferred or how disposed of, and, if the transferee is a relative or insider, the relationship, the consideration, if any, received therefor, and the disposition of such consideration).

12. Debts. (To be answered by debtor, if unmarried, otherwise for each spouse whether single or joint petition is filed).
a. Debts having Priority

(1) Nature of claim.	(2) Name of creditor and complete mailing address including zip code.	(3) Specify when claim was incurred and the consideration therefor; when claim is subject to setoff, evidenced by a judgment, negotiable instrument, or other writing, or incurred as partner or joint contractor, so indicate; specify name of any partner or joint contractor on any debt.	(4) Indicate if claim is contingent, unliquidated, or disputed.	(5) Amount of claim.
a. Wages, salary, and commissions, including vacation, severance and sick leave pay owing to employees not exceeding $2,000 to each, earned within 90 days before filing of petition or cessation of business (if earlier specify date).				
b. Contributions to employee benefit plans for services rendered within 180 before filing of petition or cessation of business (if earlier specify date).				
c. Claims of farmers, not exceeding $2,000 for each individual, pursuant to 11 U.S.C. Section 507(a)(5)(A).				
d. Claims of United States fishermen, not exceeding $2,000 for each individual, pursuant to 11 U.S.C. Section 507(a)(5)(B).				
e. Deposits by individuals, not exceeding $900 for each purchase, lease, or rental of property or services for personal, family, or household use that were not delivered or provided.				
f. Taxes owing (itemize by type of tax and taxing authority) (1) To the United States. (2) To any state. (3) To any other taxing authority				
TOTAL				

b. Secured Debts. List all debts which are or may be secured by real or personal property. (Indicate in sixth column, if debt payable in installments, the amount of each installment, the installment period (monthly, weekly, or otherwise) and number of installments in arrears, if any. Indicate in the last column whether husband or wife solely liable, or whether you are jointly liable.

(1) Creditor's name, account number and complete mailing address including zip code.	(2) Consideration or basis for debt	(3) Amount claimed by creditor	(4) If disputed, amount admitted by debtor	(5) Description of collateral (include year and make of automobile)	(6) Installment amount, period, and number of installments in arrears.	(7) Husband or wife solely liable, or jointly liable
Total secured debts						

c. Unsecured Debts. List all other debts, liquidated and unliquidated, including taxes, attorneys' fees, and tort claims.

(1) Creditor's name, account number and complete mailing address including zip code	(2) Consideration or basis for debt	(3) Amount claimed by creditor	(4) If disputed, amount admitted by debtor	(5) Husband or wife solely liable, or jointly liable
Total Unsecured Debts				

13. Codebtors. (To be answered by debtor, if unmarried, otherwise for each spouse whether single or joint petition is filed)

	Debtor.	Spouse.
a. Are any other persons liable, as cosignors, guarantors, or in any other manner, on any of the debts of either of you or is either of you so liable on the debts of others? (If so, give particulars, indicating which spouse is liable and including names of creditors, nature of debt, names and addresses of codebtors, and their relationship, if any, to you)		
b. If so, have the codebtors made any payments on the debts? (Give name of each codebtor and amount paid by codebtor)		
c. Has either of you made any payments on the debts? (If so, specify total amount paid to each creditor, whether paid by husband or wife, and name of codebtor)		

14. Property and Exemptions. (To be answered by debtor, if unmarried, otherwise for each spouse whether single or joint petition is filed)

a. Real Property. List all real property owned by either of you at date of filing of original petition. (Indicate in last column whether owned solely by husband or wife, or jointly)

(1) Description and location of property	(2) Name of any co-owner other than spouse	(3) Present market value (without deduction for mortgage or other security	(4) Amount of mortgage or other security interest on this property	(5) Name of mortgagee or other secured creditor	(6) Value claimed exempt (specify federal or state statute creating the exemption)	(7) Owned solely by husband or wife or jointly

b. Personal Property. List all other property, owned by either of you at date of filing of original petition.

(1) Description	(2) Location of property if not at debtor's residence	(3) Name of any co-owner other than spouse	(4) Present market value (without deduction for mortgage or other security interest	(5) Amount of mortgage or other security interest on this property	(6) Name of mortgagee or other secured creditor	(7) Value claimed exempt (specify federal or state statute creating the exemption	(8) Owned solely by husband or wife or jointly
Autos (give year and make)							
Household goods							
Personal effects							
Cash or finan-cial account							
Other (specify)							

UNSWORN DECLARATION UNDER PENALTY OF PERJURY

I, _____ and I, _____, declare under penalty of perjury that I have read the foregoing schedules, consisting of _____ sheets, and that they are true and correct to the best of my knowledge, information and belief.

Executed on _____, 19___.

_____
Petitioner

_____
Petitioner

UNITED STATES BANKRUPTCY COURT
_____ DISTRICT OF _____

In re _____)
_____,)
Debtor(s).)   Case No._____
)
Social Security No(s).:)
_____)

CHAPTER 13 PLAN

The debtor shall pay to the trustee out of the debtor's future earnings or other income the sum of $_____ (weekly) (semi-monthly) (monthly). From the funds received the trustee shall make distributions as follows:

1. Expenses of administration and debts entitled to priority under 11 U.S.C. Section 507.

2. Payments to secured creditors whose claims are duly filed and allowed as follows:

3. From the balance remaining after the above payments, dividends to unsecured creditors whose claims are duly filed and allowed as follows:

4. Except as provided in this plan or in the order confirming this plan, upon confirmation of this plan, all property of the estate shall vest in the debtor free and clear of any claim or interest of any creditor provided for by this plan pursuant to 11 U.S.C. Section 1327.

5. [ ] See attached addendum for additional terms.

Dated:_____

_____
Petitioner

_____
Petitioner

BANKRUPTCY PETITION COVER SHEET	CASE NUMBER

INSTRUCTIONS: This form must be completed by the debtor and submitted to the clerk of court upon the filing of the petition.

NAME OF DEBTOR (Last, First, Middle)	NAME OF JOINT DEBTOR (Spouse)
ALL OTHER NAMES, INCLUDING TRADE NAMES, USED BY THE DEBTOR IN THE LAST 6 YEARS	ALL OTHER NAMES, INCLUDING TRADE NAMES, USED BY THE JOINT DEBTOR IN THE LAST 6 YEARS
SOCIAL SECURITY NUMBER	SOCIAL SECURITY NUMBER
ADDRESS OF DEBTOR (Street, City, State, Zip Code)	ADDRESS OF JOINT DEBTOR
NAME OF COUNTY	NAME OF COUNTY

TYPE OF PETITION Voluntary Petition. CHAPTER OF BANKRUPTCY CODE UNDER WHICH PETITION IS FILED (Check one box) ☐ Chapter 7 ☐ Chapter 13	NATURE OF DEBT Non-business/Consumer

ESTIMATED NUMBER OF CREDITORS ☐1-15 ☐16-49 ☐50-99 ☐100-999	☐ No assets will be available for distribution to creditors. ☐ Assets will be available for distribution to creditors.

ESTIMATED ASSETS (IN THOUSANDS OF DOLLARS)

☐ Under 50   ☐ 50-99   ☐ 100-499

ESTIMATED LIBILITIES (IN THOUSANDS OF DOLLARS)

☐ Under 50   ☐ 50-99   ☐ 100-499

☐ No Attorney

FILING FEE (Check one box) ☐ Filing Fee Attached. ☐ Filing fee to be paid in installments. Application Attached.

RELATED BANKRUPTCY CASE (IF ANY)		
DEBTOR		CASE NO.
DISTRICT	DIVISIONAL OFFICE	NAME OF JUDGE
DATE	PRINT NAME	SIGNATURE OF ATTORNEY (OR DEBTOR)

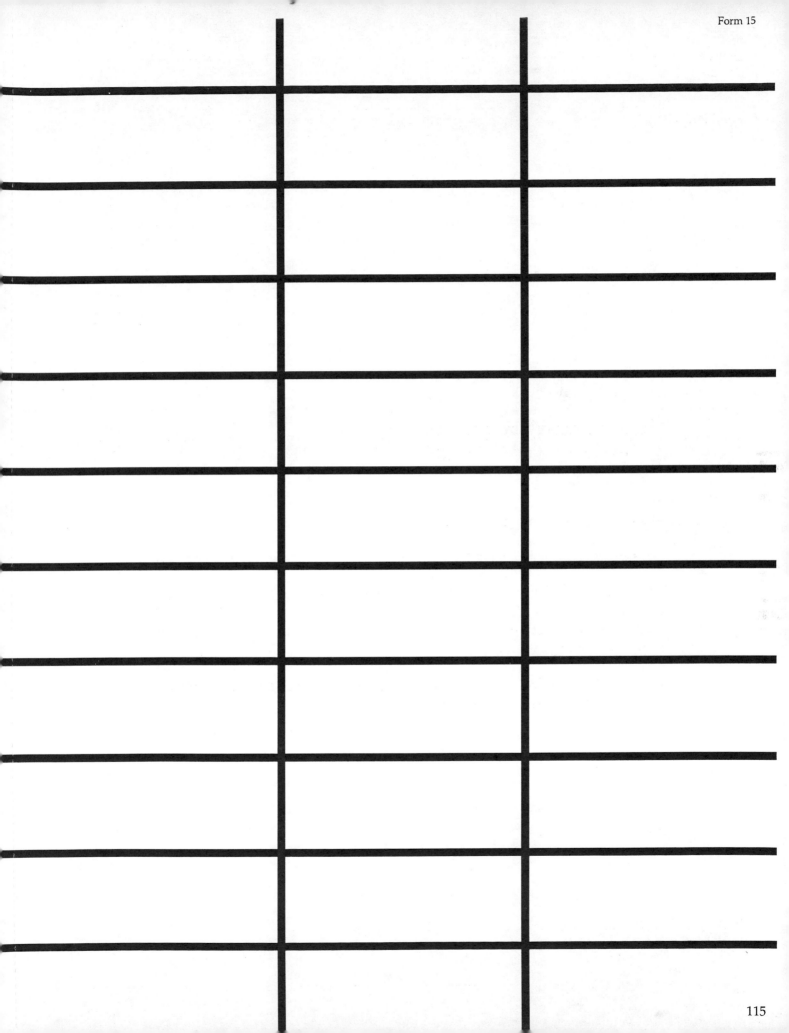

Dear Sir or Madam:

YOU ARE HEREBY ADVISED that on _____,
I filed a voluntary petition with the U.S. Bankruptcy Court, in case
number _____. Pursuant to the U.S. Bankruptcy
Code, you may not:

-Take any action to evict me from my residence.

-Discontinue any service or benefit being provided to me.

-Take any action against me or my property to collect any debt.

-Enforce any lien on my real or personal property, or repossess
any of my property.

Any violation of these prohibitions may constitute contempt of
court and be punished accordingly.

Sincerely,

```
                              )
                              )
                              )
                              )
                              )
        vs.                   )   Case No._____
                              )
                              )
                              )
                              )
```

SUGGESTION OF BANKRUPTCY

The Defendant(s),_____, hereby notifies this Court that said defendant(s) filed a Petition for Bankruptcy, in the United States District Court on _____, a copy of said petition is attached hereto.

Dated: _____   Signed: _____
                                            Defendant

                                            _____
                                            Defendant

CERTIFICATE OF SERVICE

I hereby certify that a copy of the foregoing was sent by first class, U. S. Mail on _____, to the following parties:

                                            _____

UNITED STATES BANKRUPTCY COURT
_____ DISTRICT OF _____

In re _____)
_____,)
Debtor(s).   )   Case No._____
)
Social Security No(s):   )
_____   )

CERTIFICATE OF MAILING

I hereby certify that a copy of the following documents:

was sent by first class, U. S. Mail on _____, to the following:

DATED:_____   _____

CERTIFIED MAIL
RETURN RECEIPT REQUESTED
No._____

Dear Sir or Madam:

My current financial situation may require me to file for bank-ruptcy protection. In order to avoid this, I am requesting that my payments on your account be restructured. This will allow me to pay you the full amount you are owed.

My net monthly income is $_____. After paying essential ex-penses, such as housing, utilities, food, clothing, transportation for work, and medical expenses, I am left with a monthly disposable income of $_____. Out of this balance I am able to pay my creditors as follows:

CREDITOR   OLD AMOUNT   REVISED AMOUNT

This schedule represents an equal pro-rata reduction for each unsecured creditor. Please let me know if this new arrangement is acceptable. Unless I hear from you before the next payment is due, I will assume this proposal is acceptable, and will make my next payment according to the revised amount.

Thank you for your attention to this matter.

Sincerely,

MONTHLY BUDGET

TOTAL MONTHLY INCOME   _____

EXPENSES (Monthly):

Mortgage or Rent   _____
Homeowners/Renters Insurance   _____
Real Estate Taxes   _____
Electricity   _____
Gas   _____
Water   _____
Telephone   _____
Garbage Pick-up   _____
Other:_____   _____
Home Repair/Maintenance   _____
Auto Loan   _____
Other Installment Loan Payments:

_____   _____
_____   _____
_____   _____
_____   _____
_____   _____

Auto Insurance   _____
Gasoline   _____
Auto Repairs/Maintenance   _____
Food   _____
Clothing   _____
Medical, Dental, and Medicines   _____
Life Insurance   _____
Laundry   _____
Recreation/Travel/Entertainment   _____
Education   _____
License Fees, Dues, Memberships   _____
Other Taxes   _____
Other:_____   _____

_____   _____
_____   _____
_____   _____
_____   _____

TOTAL MONTHLY EXPENSES $_____

UNITED STATES BANKRUPTCY COURT
_____ DISTRICT OF _____

In re _____)
_____,)
Debtor(s).   )   Case No._____
)
Social Security No(s).:   )
_____   )

AMENDMENT COVER SHEET

The Debtor hereby files the attached amended documents, consisting of :

[ ] Petition Cover Sheet

[ ] Schedule A   [ ] Schedule B   [ ] Summary of Debts and Assets

[ ] Schedule of Current Income and Expenditures

[ ] Statement of Financial Affairs   [ ] Statement of Intention

[ ] Chapter 13 Statement   [ ] Chapter 13 Plan

UNSWORN DECLARATION UNDER PENALTY OF PERJURY

I, _____ and I, _____, declare under penalty of perjury that

the information set forth above, and contained in the attached amended documents, consisting

of _____ pages, is true and correct to the best of my (our) information and belief.

Dated:_____

_____
Petitioner

_____
Petitioner

UNITED STATES BANKRUPTCY COURT
_____ DISTRICT OF _____

In re _____)
_____,)
Debtor(s).)   Case No._____
)
Social Security No(s).:)
_____)

MOTION TO CONVERT TO CHAPTER 7

The Debtor, having originally filed this action pursuant to Chapter 13 of the U.S. Bankruptcy Code, hereby moves this court to convert this action to a proceeding pursuant to Chapter 7 of the U. S. Bankruptcy Code. In furtherance of this motion the Debtor has attached the following documents hereto: Schedules A and B, Summary of Debts and Property, Schedule of Current Income and Expenditures for Individual Debtor, Chapter 7 Individual Debtor's Statement of Intention, and Statement of Executory Contracts.

Dated:_____   _____
                                                Petitioner

                                                _____
                                                Petitioner

ORDER

IN CONSIDERATION of the foregoing motion of the Debtor,

IT IS HEREBY ORDERED, that this action is converted to a proceeding pursuant to Chapter 7 of the U. S. Bankruptcy Code.

Dated:_____   _____
                                                Judge

APPENDIX B: LOCAL EXEMPTIONS (BY STATE)

This Appendix is used to find what exemptions are available to you. In addition to listing the exemptions available in each state, the Federal exemptions are also listed. The Federal exemptions are not available in all states, so check the list at the beginning of the Federal exemption section. If the Federal exemptions are allowed in your state, compare the exemptions in your state to the Federal exemptions to determine which way will allow you to keep more property. In most cases the state exemptions will be better for you, but make the comparison just to be sure. Ther is also a listing of "Federal Non-Bankruptcy Exemptions." These are available also, but only if you use your state's exemptions.

The following listings give the section number for the applicable state law, and the exemption that relates to that section. You will need the statute reference in order to complete Schedule B-4 (which is part of FORM 7). At the beginning of each state's section, you will find an example of how to write the statute reference in Column (3) of Schedule B-4. If no amount is stated, the amount of that type of property you may claim is unlimited. Where an amount is stated, you may only claim up to that amount as exempt. If you want to be sure you understand the exemption, go to your library and look up the actual language in that section of your state's law. Many state's laws have volume numbers on them. Where applicable, advice is given to ignore the volume number because it is not part of the official manner of referring to the law in your state. Refer to part F. in Section 9 of this book for more information about statutes and legal research. Otherwise, you can claim the exemption and see if the trustee allows it.

DOUBLING EXEMPTIONS. Some states allow a husband and wife to each claim a separate exemption. For example, if an automobile is exempt up to $3,000 in equity, the husband and wife may each claim an auto up to $3,000. This is referred to as "doubling" the exemption. An asterisk (*) after an item indicates that doubling is specifically prohibited by law. Two asterisks (**) indicates that doubling is specifically approved by law. No notation indicates that the law does not state whether doubling is permitted, so you may want to list the exemption for both husband and wife, and see if the trustee accepts it.

"ERISA" BENEFITS. These are benefits from retirement plans which qualify under the federal ERISA act. Several states have laws providing for a bankruptcy exemption for ERISA-qualified retirement plan benefits. However, the U.S. Supreme Court has declared such state exemptions to be invalid. This has an impact in the following states (section numbers of the state law are in parentheses): Alaska (9.38.017); Arizona (33-1126); California-System 2 (703.140); Connecticut (52-352b); Florida (222.21); Georgia (18-4-22.1); Hawaii (36-651-124); Idaho (55-1201A); Illinois (110-12-1001); Kansas (60-2308); Louisiana (20:33); Maine (14-4422); Mississippi (85-3-1); Missouri (513.430); New York (Debtor & Creditor 282); North Dakota (28-22-03.1); Ohio (2329.66); Oklahoma (31-1); Oregon (23.170); South Carolina (15-41-30); Tennessee (26-2-111); Texas (Property 42.0021); and West Virginia (38-10-4). This court decision may affect the exemptions of many retirement plans in all states, and the full ramifications are not completely known. The Supreme Court, in an example of how across-the-board application of law can lead to an absurd result, decided that only the Federal Bankruptcy Exemption is allowed with respect to ERISA plan benefits. You may want to check with the trustee, if you have an ERISA-qualified retirement plan.

WARNING: THE FOLLOWING EXEMPTION CHARTS ARE NOT GUARANTEED TO BE CURRENT, NOR ARE THEY GUARANTEED TO CONTAIN EVERY POSSIBLE EXEMPTION. THESE CHARTS ARE DESIGNED TO INCLUDE THE BASIC EXEMPTIONS TO COVER THE MOST USUAL SITUATIONS. LEGISLATURES MAY CHANGE THE EXEMPTIONS AT ANY TIME, AND THERE MAY BE OBSCURE EXEMPTIONS APPLICABLE TO VERY NARROW SITUATIONS. YOUR LOCAL PUBLIC LIBRARY, OR LAW LIBRARY (usually found at your county courthouse) SHOULD HAVE A CURRENT COPY OF YOUR STATE'S LAWS. IF YOU THINK YOU HAVE A PARTICULAR ASSET WHICH MAY BE ENTITLED TO AN EXEMPTION, OR FEEL YOU NEED AN EXEMPTION EXPLAINED IN MORE DETAIL, YOU SHOULD CONSULT AN ATTORNEY.

FEDERAL BANKRUPTCY EXEMPTIONS

The following exemptions are available if you live in one of the following states:

Connecticut	Massachusetts	New Jersey	Rhode Island	Washington
District of Columbia	Michigan	New Mexico	Texas	Wisconsin
Hawaii	Minnesota	Pennsylvania	Vermont	

If you use these exemptions, however, you may not use the exemptions listed under your state. Be sure to compare these exemptions to those in the listing for your state, and use whichever allows you to keep more of your property.

The following section numbers relate to Title 11 of the United States Code, which is abbreviated "11 U.S.C." followed by the appropriate section number. An example is: 11 U.S.C. Section 522(d)(1). Only the section number is used below.

HOMESTEAD
522(d)(1)   Real property, up to $7,500. Unused portion, up to $3,750, may be used for other property.

PERSONAL PROPERTY
522(d)(2)   Motor vehicle up to $1,200.
522(d)(3)   Animals, crops, clothing, appliances and furnishings, books, household goods, and musical instruments up to $200 per item, and up to $4,000 total.
522(d)(4)   Jewelry up to $500.
522(d)(9)   Health aids.
522(d)(11)(B) Wrongful death recovery for person you depended upon.
522(d)(11)(D) Personal injury recovery up to $7,500, except for pain and suffering or for pecuniary loss.
522(d)(11)(E) Lost earning payments.

PENSIONS
522(d)(10)(E) ERISA-qualified benefits needed for support.

PUBLIC BENEFITS
522(d)(10)(A) Public assistance, Social security, Veteran's benefits, Unemployment Compensation.
522(d)(11)(A) Crime victim's compensation.

TOOLS OF TRADE
522(d)(6)   Implements, books and tools of trade, up to $750.

ALIMONY AND CHILD SUPPORT
522(d)(10)(D) Alimony and child support needed for support.
INSURANCE
522(d)(7)   Unmatured life insurance policy.
522(d)(8)   Life insurance policy with loan value up to $4,000.
522(d)(10)(C) Disability, unemployment or illness benefits.
522(d)(11)(C) Life insurance payments for a person you depended on, which you need for support.

MISCELLANEOUS
522(d)(5) $400 of any property, and unused portion of homestead up to $3,750.

FEDERAL NON-BANKRUPTCY EXEMPTIONS
You may only use these exemptions if you choose the exemption listed under your state. You may not use these if you choose to use the Federal Bankruptcy Exemptions.

RETIREMENT BENEFITS
50 U.S.C. s.403	CIA employees
5 U.S.C. s.8346	Civil Service employees
22 U.S.C. s.4060	Foreign service employees
10 U.S.C. s.1440	Military service employees
45 U.S.C. s.231m	Railroad workers
42 U.S.C. s.407	Social security benefits
38 U.S.C. s.3101	Veteran's benefits

SURVIVOR'S BENEFITS
10 U.S.C. s.1450	Military service
28 U.S.C. s.376	Judges, U.S. court directors
33 U.S.C. s.775	Lighthouse workers

DEATH AND DISABILITY BENEFITS
5 U.S.C. s.8130	U.S. Government employees
33 U.S.C. s.916	Longshoremen, harbor workers
42 U.S.C. s.1717	Military service

MISCELLANEOUS
10 U.S.C. s.1035	Military deposits to savings accounts (while on permanent duty outside the U.S.).
15 U.S.C. s.1673	75% of earned but unpaid wages (Judge may approve more).
25 U.S.C. s.543 & 545	Klamath Indians tribe benefits.
38 U.S.C. s.770(g)	Military group life insurance.
45 U.S.C. s.352(e)	Railroad workers' unemployment.
46 U.S.C. s.11110	Seamen's clothing.
46 U.S.C. s.11111	Seamen's wages (while on a voyage and pursuant to a written contract).

ALABAMA   References are to the Code of Alabama. Example: "C.A. s.6-10-2". Ignore volume numbers; look for "title" numbers.

HOMESTEAD
6-10-2   Real property or mobile home, up to $5,000, property can't exceed 160 acres. (**)

PERSONAL PROPERTY
6-10-5   A burial place and a church pew or seat.
6-10-6   Clothing, books and family portraits and pictures, and $3,000 of any other personal property.

WAGES
6-10-7   75% of earned but unpaid wages.

PENSIONS
12-18-10   Judges.
16-25-23   Teachers.
36-21-77   Law enforcement officers.
36-27-28   State employees.

PUBLIC BENEFITS
15-23-15   Crime victims' compensation.
25-4-140   Unemployment compensation.
25-5-86   Workers' compensation.
25-5-179   Coal miners' pneumoconiosis benefits.
31-7-2   Southeast Asian War POW's benefits.
38-4-8   AFDC and aid to blind, aged, and disabled.

TOOLS OF TRADE
31-2-78   Arms, uniforms and equipment required to be kept by state military personnel.

INSURANCE
6-10-8;
27-14-29   Life insurance proceeds if beneficiary is spouse or child of the insured.
27-14-31   Disability proceeds up to an average of $250 per month.

ALASKA   References are to the Alaska Statutes. Example: "A.S. s.9.38.010". Ignore volume numbers; look for "title" numbers.

HOMESTEAD
9.38-010   Up to $54,000 total, even for husband and wife filing jointly.

PERSONAL PROPERTY
9.38.015   A burial plot and needed health aids.
9.38.020   Motor vehicle up to $3,000; pets up to $1,000; jewelry up to $1,000; and household goods, clothing, books, musical instruments, and family portraits and heirlooms up to $3,000.
9.38.030   Personal injury and wrongful death recoveries.

WAGES
9.38.030;
9.38.050   Weekly net earnings up to $350, or up to $550 if sole wage earner in a household.

PENSIONS
9.38.015   Public employees and teachers pensions building up.

9.38.030   Payments being received from other pensions.

PUBLIC BENEFITS
9.38.015   Alaska longevity bonus, crime victims' compensation and federally exempt public benefits.
23.20.405   Unemployment compensation.
23.30.160   Workers' compensation.
47.25.210   General relief assistance.
47.25.395   AFDC
47.25.550   Assistance to blind, elderly and disabled adults.

TOOLS OF TRADE
9.38.020   Implements, books or tools up to $2,800.

ALIMONY AND CHILD SUPPORT
9.38.015   Child support if received from a collection agency.
9.38.030   Alimony

INSURANCE
9.38.015; 9.38.020
            Medical and disability benefits.
9.38.025   Life insurance or annuity contracts up to a $10,000 loan value.

125

ARIZONA   References are to the Arizona Revised Statutes. Example: "A.R.S. s.33-1101". Ignore volume numbers; look for "section" numbers.

HOMESTEAD

33-1101	Up to $5,000. No doubling. Includes sale proceeds up to 18 months after sale.

PERSONAL PROPERTY (**)

33-123	The following items up to $4,000 total: Two beds plus an additional bed for each additional member of the family; one bed table, dresser and lamp for each bed; bedding; kitchen table; dining table and 4 chairs plus an additional chair for each additional member of the family; living room chair for each member of the family; couch; 3 living room tables and lamps; living room carpet or rug; refrigerator; stove; washer and dryer; one TV, radio or stereo (not one of each); alarm clock; vacuum cleaner; family portraits; and any pictures, paintings, and drawings created by the debtor.
33-124	Food and fuel for 6 months.
33-125	Motor vehicle up to $1,500 (or $4,000 if disabled); clothing to $500; pets, horses, milk cows and poultry to $500; books to $250; wedding and engagement rings to $1,000; musical instruments to $250; watch to $100; wheelchair and prostheses; and up to $500 total for bicycle, sewing machine, typewriter, burial plot, firearm and bible (only one of each may be kept).
33-126	Proceeds for sold or damaged exempt property; prepaid rent or security deposit to lesser of $1,000 or 1.5 times rent (only if not claiming homestead); bank deposit to $150 in one account.

WAGES

33-1131	Minimum of 75% of unpaid net wages or pension payments. Judge may allow more.

PENSIONS

9-931	Police officers.
9-968	Firefighters.
15-1628	Members of board of regents.
38-762	State employees.
38-811	Elected officials.
38-850	Public safety personnel.
41-955	Rangers.

PUBLIC BENEFITS

23-783	Unemployment compensation.
23-1068	Workers' compensation.
46-208	Welfare benefits.

TOOLS OF TRADE

33-1127	Teaching aids of a teacher.
33-1130 (**)	Tools, equipment and books up to $2,500; Farm machinery, utensils, instruments of husbandry, feed, seed, grain and animals up to a total value of $2,500; and arms, uniforms and equipment you are required by law to keep.

INSURANCE

20-881	Fraternal benefit society benefits.
20-1131	Life insurance cash value up to $2,000 per dependent/$10,000 total.
20-1132	Group life insurance policy or proceeds.
33-1126 (**)	Life insurance proceeds if beneficiary is spouse or child, up to $20,000; life insurance cash value to $1,000 per dependent/$5,000 total; and health, accident or disability benefits.

ARKANSAS   References are to the Arkansas Code of 1987 Annotated. Example: "A.C.A. s.16-66-210". Ignore volume numbers; look for "chapter" numbers.

HOMESTEAD (Choose one of the following)

16-66-210 (*)	Head of family may claim: Real or personal property used as a residence; of up to 1/4 acre in a city, town, or village; or up to 80 acres elsewhere. If between 1/4 and 1 acre in city, etc., or 80 to 160 acres elsewhere, amount of exemption in limited to $2,500. No homestead may exceed 1 acre in city, etc., or 160 acres elsewhere. This exemption is also found in the State Constitution, and the reference to "Ark. Const. 9-3, 9-4, & 9-5" should also be used.
16-66-218	Real or personal property used as a residence, up to $800 if single or $1,250 if married.

PERSONAL PROPERTY

16-66-218	Motor vehicle up to $1,200, and wedding bands provided that any diamond can't exceed 1/2 carat.
16-66-207	Burial plot up to 5 acres, provided you don't use the homestead exemption in section 16-66-218.
Ark. Const.	Clothing of unlimited value; and any personal property of up to $500 if married or head of family, or $200 otherwise. Use reference to "Ark. Const. 9-1 &9-2".

WAGES

16-66-208	Earned but unpaid wages due for 60 days, but in no event less than $25 per week.

PENSIONS

16-66-218	IRA deposits up to $20,000 if deposited over 1 year before filing for bankruptcy.
24-6-223	State police officers.
24-7-715	School employees.
24-10-616	Police officers and firefighters.
24-11-417	Disabled police officers.
24-11-814	Disabled firefighters.

PUBLIC BENEFITS

11-9-110	Worker's compensation.
11-10-109	Unemployment compensation.
16-90-716	Crime victims' compensation, unless you are seeking to discharge a debt for treatment of an injury incurred during the crime.
20-76-430	AFDC, and aid to blind, aged or disabled.

TOOLS OF TRADE

16-66-218	Tools, books and implements of trade to $750.

INSURANCE

16-66-209	Life, health, accident of disability proceeds, whether paid or due.
23-71-112	Stipulated insurance premiums.
23-72-114	Mutual assessment life or disability benefits up to $1,000.
23-74-119	Fraternal benefit society benefits.
23-79-131	Life insurance proceeds if beneficiary isn't the insured; life insurance proceeds if policy prohibits proceeds from being used to pay beneficiary's creditors.
23-79-132	Group life insurance.
23-79-133	Disabliity benefits.
23-79-134	Annuity contract.

CALIFORNIA California has two separate systems of exemptions. You must select one of the two. You cannot mix exemptions from the two systems. References are to the California Code of Civil Procedure. Example: "Cal. Code Civ. Proc. s.704.710".

CALIFORNIA (SYSTEM 1)

HOMESTEAD

704.710 & 704.730 Real or personal property occupied at time of filing for bankruptcy, including mobile home, boat, stock cooperative, community apartment, planned development or condominium, up to the following limits: $30,000 if single and not disables; $45,000 if family and no other member has homestead; $75,000 if 65 or older or if physically or mentally disabled; $75,000 if creditors are seeking to force sale of your home and you are either (a)55 or older, single and earn under $15,000 per year, or (b)55 or older, married and earn under $20,000 per year. Sale proceeds are exempt for up to 6 months after sale.*

PERSONAL PROPERTY

704.010	Motor vehicle or insurance if vehicle lost, destroyed or damaged up to $1,200.
704.020	Food, clothing, appliances and furnishings.
704.030	Building materials to repair or improve home up to $1,000.
704.040	Jewelry, heirlooms and art up to $2,500 total.
704.050	Health aids.
704.080	Bank deposits from Social Security Administration up to $500 for single payee, and $750 for more than one payee; proceeds from exempt property in form of cash or bank deposits.
704.140	Personal injury causes of action, and recoveries needed for support.
704.150	Wrongful death causes of action, and recoveries needed for support.
704.200	Burial plot

WAGES

704.070	75% of wages paid within 30 days prior to filing bankruptcy.
704.113	Public employee vacation credits.

PENSIONS

704.110	Public retirement benefits.
704.115	Private retirements benefits to extent tax-deferred, including IRA & Keogh.

PUBLIC BENEFITS

704.120	Unemployment benefits and union benefits due to labor dispute.
704.160	Workers' compensation.
704.170	AFDC and aid to blind, aged and disabled.
704.180	Relocation benefits.
704.190	Financial aid to students.

TOOLS OF TRADE

704.060	Tools, implements, materials, books, uniforms, instruments, equipment, furnishings, motor vehicle, and vessel up to $2,500, or up to $5,000 if used by both spouses in the same occupation. Can't claim motor vehicle here if already claimed under 704.010.

INSURANCE

704.100 (**)	Matured life insurance benefits needed for support of unlimited value, unmatured life insurance policy up to $4,000 in value, and fraternal life insurance benefits to $4,000.
704.120	Fraternal unemployment benefits.
704.130	Disability or health benefits.
704.720	Homeowners' insurance proceeds for 6 months after received, up to amount of homestead limit.
Other	Fidelity bonds. Refer to as "Labor 404".
Other	Life insurance proceeds if policy prohibits use to pay creditors. Refer to as "Ins. 10132, 10170 & 10171".

CALIFORNIA (SYSTEM 2)

HOMESTEAD

703.140(b)(1)	Real or personal property used as a residence up to $7,500. Any unused portion of the $7,500 may be applied to any property.

PERSONAL PROPERTY

703.140(b)(1)	Burial plot up to $7,500, instead of homestead.
703.140(b)(2)	Motor vehicle up to $1,200.
703.140(b)(3)	Clothing, household goods, appliances, furnishings, animals, books, musical instruments and crops up to $200 per item.
703.140(b)(4)	Jewelry up to $500.
703.140(b)(9)	Health aids.
703.140(b)(11)(B)	Wrongful death recoveries needed for support.
703.140(b)(11)(D,E)	Personal injury recoveries up to $7,500, not to include pain, suffering or pecuniary loss.

PUBLIC BENEFITS

703.140(b)(10)(A)	Unemployment compensation, social security, and public assistance.
703.140(b)(10)(B)	Veterans' benefits.
703.140(b)(11)(A)	Crime victims' compensation.

TOOLS OF TRADE

703.140(b)(6)	Tools, books and implements of trade up to $750.

ALIMONY AND CHILD SUPPORT

703.140(b)(10)(D)	Alimony and child support needed for support.

INSURANCE

703.140(b)(7)	Unmatured life insurance policy, other than credit.
703.140(b)(8)	Unmatured life insurance contract accrued interest, dividends, loan, cash or surrender value up to $4,000.
703.140(b)(10)(C)	Disability benefits.
703.140(b)(11)(C)	Life insurance proceeds needed for support.
Other	Fidelity bonds. Refer to as "Labor 404".

MISCELLANEOUS

703.140(b)(5)	$7,900 of any property, less any claim for homestead or burial plot.

COLORADO   References are to the Colorado Revised Statutes Annotated. Example: "C.R.S.A. s.13-54-102".

HOMESTEAD

13-54-102   Mobile home used as residence up to $6,000 value; house trailer or coach used as residence up to $3,500.

38-41-201   Real property, including mobile or manufactured home if loan incurred after 1/1/83, up to $20,000.
For homestead exemption, must be occupied at time petition is filed. Sale proceeds are exempt for 1 year after sale. Spouse or child of deceased owner can also qualify.

PERSONAL PROPERTY

13-54-102   Motor vehicles to $1,000 to get to work (up to $3,000 to get medical care if elderly or disabled); clothing to $750; health aids; household goods to $1,500; food and fuel to $300; 1 burial plot per person; jewelry and articles of adornment to $500 total; pictures and books to $750; security deposit; proceeds for damaged exempt property; personal injury recoveries, unless debt related to the injury.

WAGES

13-54-104   Minimum 75% of earned but unpaid wages, and pension payments. Judge may approve more for low income debtors.

PENSIONS

22-64-120   Teachers.
24-51-212   Public employees.
31-30-313;
31-30-616   Police officers.

31-30-412;
31-30-518   Firefighters.

PUBLIC BENEFITS

8-80-103   Unemployment compensation.
8-52-107   Workers' compensation.
13-54-102   Veterans' benefits for veteran, spouse or child if veteran served in war.
13-54-102;
24-4.1-114   Crime victims' compensation.
26-2-131   AFDC, aid to blind, aged and disabled.

TOOLS OF TRADE

13-54-102   Stock in trade, supplies, fixtures, machines, tools, maps, equipment and books to $1,500 total; library of a professional to $1,500; livestock and poultry of a farmer to $3,000; horses, mules, wagons, carts, machinery, harness and tools of farmer to $2,000 total.

INSURANCE

10-7-106   Life insurance proceeds if policy prohibits use to pay creditors.
10-7-205   Group life insurance policy or proceeds.
10-8-114   Disability benefits up to $200 per month.
10-14-122   Fraternal benefit society benefits.
13-54-102   Life insurance dividends, interest, cash or surrender value up to $5,000.
38-41-209   Homeowners' insurance proceeds for 1 year after received up to $20,000.

CONNECTICUT   References are to the Connecticut General Statutes Annotated. Example: "C.G.S.A. s.52-352b". Ignore volume numbers; look for "title" numbers.

PERSONAL PROPERTY

52-352b   Motor vehicle up to $1,500; food, clothing and health aids; appliances, furniture and bedding; wedding and engagement rings; burial plot; residential utility and security deposits for 1 residence; proceeds for damaged exempt property.

WAGES

52-361a   Minimum 75% of earned but unpaid wages. Judge may approve more for low income debtors.

PENSIONS

5-171;5-192w   State employees.
10-183q   Teachers.

PUBLIC BENEFITS

31-272;
52-352b   Unemployment compensation.
52-352b   Workers' compensation; veterans' benefits; social security; wages from earnings incentive programs; AFDC; aid to blind, aged and disabled.
52-352b;
54-213   Crime victims' compensation.

TOOLS OF TRADE

52-352b   Arms, military equipment, uniforms and musical instruments of military personnel; tools, books, instruments and farm animals needed.

ALIMONY AND CHILD SUPPORT

52-352b   Alimony and child support.

INSURANCE

38-161   Life insurance proceeds, dividends, interest, or cash or surrender value.
38-162   Life insurance proceeds if policy prohibits use to pay creditors.
38-229   Fraternal benefit society benefits.
38-336   Benefits under no-fault insurance law.
52-352b   Health and disability benefits; disability benefits paid by association for it members.

DELAWARE   References are to the Delaware Code Annotated. Example: "D.C.A. s.10-4902". Ignore volume numbers; look for "title" numbers.

LIMITATION: Total exemptions for a single person may not exceed $5,000; and for husband and wife may not exceed $10,000.

HOMESTEAD: None; although case law has made some tenancies by the entirety exempt without limitation.

PERSONAL PROPERTY
10-4902   Clothing, including jewelry; books; family pictures; piano; leased organs and sewing machines; burial plot; church pew or any seat in public place of worship. Also $500 of any other personal property if head of family.

WAGES
10-4913   85% of earned but unpaid wages.

PENSIONS
9-4316   Kent County employees.
11-8803   Police officers.
16-6653   Volunteer firefighters.
29-5503   State employees.

PUBLIC BENEFITS
19-2355   Workers' compensation.
19-3374   Unemployment compensation.
31-513   General assistance; AFDC; aid to aged and disabled.
31-2309   Aid to blind.

TOOLS OF TRADE
10-4902   Tools, implements and fixtures, up to $75 in New Castle and Sussex counties, and up to $50 in Kent County.

INSURANCE
12-1901   Employee life insurance benefits.
18-2726   Health or disability benefits.
18-2727   Group life insurance policy or proceeds.
18-2728   Annuity contract proceeds up to $350 per month.
18-2729   Life insurance proceeds if policy prohibits use to pay creditors.
18-6118   Fraternal benefit society benefits.

DISTRICT OF COLUMBIA   References are to the D.C. Code. Example: "D.C.C. s.45-1869". Ignore volume number; look for "title" number.

HOMESTEAD
45-1869   Residential condominium deposit. Case law has allowed some tenancies by the entirety exempt without limit.

PERSONAL PROPERTY
15-501   Clothing up to $300 (also refer to 15-503); beds, bedding, radios, cooking utensils, stoves, furniture, furnishings and sewing machines up to $300 total; books to $400; family pictures; food and fuel to last 3 months.
29-1128   Cooperative association holding to $50.

WAGES
15-503   Non-wage, earnings, including pensions, for 60 days up to $200 per month for head of family, or $60 per month otherwise.
16-572   Minimum 75% of earned but unpaid wages or pension payments.

PENSIONS
11-1570   Judges.
31-1217;31-1238 Public school teachers.

PUBLIC BENEFITS
3-215.1   General assistance; AFDC; aid to blind, aged and disabled.

3-407   Crime victims' compensation.
36-317   Workers' compensation.
46-119   Unemployment compensation.

TOOLS OF TRADE
1-806   Seal and documents of notary public.
15-501   Motor vehicle, cart, wagon or dray, horse or mule harness up to $500; stock and materials to $200; library, furniture, tools of professional or artist to $300.
15-501;15-503   Mechanic's tools, tools of trade or business to $200.

INSURANCE
15-503   Other insurance proceeds to $200 per month, for a maximum of 2 months, for head of family; up to $60 per month otherwise.
35-521   Life insurance proceeds, dividends, interest, cash or surrender value.
35-522   Disability benefits.
35-523   Group life insurance policy or proceeds.
35-525   Life insurance proceeds if policy prohibits use to pay creditors.
35-1211   Fraternal benefit society benefits.

FLORIDA   References are to the Florida Statutes. Example: "F.S. s. 222.05". Ignore volume numbers; look for "chapter" numbers.

HOMESTEAD

222.05   Real or personal property, including mobile or modular home and condominium, to unlimited value. Property cannot exceed 1/2 acre in a municipality, or 160 acres elsewhere. Spouse or child of deceased owner may claim exemption. (Also refer to Florida Constitution, as "Fla. Const. 10-4.").

PERSONAL PROPERTY

Other   Any personal property up to $1,000 total. (Refer to as "Fla. Const. 10-4").(**)

WAGES

222.11   Earned but unpaid wages, or wages paid and in a bnak account, only if head of household.

222.21   Federal government employees pension payments needed for support and received 3 months before filing bankruptcy.

PENSIONS

121.131   State officers and employees.
122.15   County officers and employees.
175.241   Firefighters.
185.25   Police officers.
238.15   Teachers.
321.22   Highway patrol officers.

PUBLIC BENEFITS

222.201   Public assistance and social security.
222.201;443.051   Unemployment compensation.
222.201;744.626   Veterans' benefits.
440.22   Workers' compensation.
960.14   Crime victims' compensation unless seeking to discharge debt for treatment of crime related unjury.

TOOLS OF TRADE: None.

ALIMONY AND CHILD SUPPORT

222.201   Alimony and child support needed for support.

INSURANCE

222.13   Death benefits payable to a specific beneficiary.
222.14   Annuity contract proceeds and life insuramce cash surrender value.
222.18   Disability or illness benefits.
632.619   Fraternal benefit society benefits, if received before 10/1/96.

GEORGIA   References are to the Official Code of Georgia Annotated (not the Georgia Code). Example: "C.G.A. s. 44-13-100". Ignore volume numbers; look for "title" numbers.

HOMESTEAD

44-13-100   Real or personal property, including coop, used as a residence up to $5,000. Unused portion may be applied to any other property.

PERSONAL PROPERTY

44-13-100   Motor vehicles up to $1,000; clothing, household goods, appliances, furnishings, books, musical instruments, animals and crops up to $200 per item, and $3,500 total; jewelry up to $500; health aids; lost future earnings needed for support; personal injury recoveries up to $7,500; wrongful death recoveries needed for support. Also, burial plot in lieu of homestead.

WAGES

18-4-20   Minimum 75% of earned but unpaid wages for private and federal government workers. Judge may approve more for low income debtors.

PENSIONS

47-2-332   Public employees.
44-13-100   Other pensions needed for support, but only as to payments being received.

PUBLIC BENEFITS

44-13-100   Unemployment compensation, veterans' benefits, social security, crime victims' compensation, and local public assistance.
49-4-35   Old age assistance.
49-4-58   Aid to blind.
49-4-84   Workers' compensation; aid to disabled.

TOOLS OF TRADE

44-13-100   Tools, books and implements of trade up to $500.

ALIMONY AND CHILD SUPPORT

44-13-100   Alimony and child support needed for support.

INSURANCE

44-13-100   Unmatured life insurance contract, unmatured life insurance dividends, interest, loan value or cash value up to $2,000 if you or someone you depend on is beneficiary, life insurance proceeds if policy is owned by someone you depend on and is needed for support.
33-15-20   Fraternal benefit society benefits.
33-25-11   Life insurance proceeds, dividends, interest, loan, cash or surrender value, provided that beneficiary is not the insured.
33-28-7   Annuity and endowment contract benefits.
33-27-7   Group insurance.
33-26-5   Industrial life insurance policy owned by someone you depend on for support.
33-29-15   Disability or health benefits up to $250 per month.

HAWAII

References are to Hawaii Revised Statutes. Example: "H.R.S. 36-651-92". Ignore volume numbers; look for "title" numbers.

HOMESTEAD

36-651-92 — Up to $30,000 if head of family or over 65; up to $20,000 otherwise. Sale proceeds are exempt for 6 months after sale. Some tenancies by the entirety are exempt without limit.

PERSONAL PROPERTY

20-359-104 — Down payment for home in state project.

36-651-121 — Motor vehicle up to wholesale value of $1,000; clothing; appliances and furnishings needed; books; jewelry and articles of adornment up to $1,000; proceeds for sold or damaged exempt property (sale proceeds exempt for 6 months after sale); burial plot up to 250 square feet, plus on-site tombstones, monuments and fencing

WAGES

20-353-22 — Prisoner's wages held by DSSH.

36-651-121;

36-652-1 — Unpaid wages due for services of the past 31 days. If more than 31 days, 95% of first $100, 90% of second $100, and 80% of balance.

PENSIONS

7-88-91;

36-653-3 — Public officers and employees.

7-88-169 — Police officers and firefighters.

PUBLIC BENEFITS

20-346-33 — Public assistance paid by DSSH

21-383-163 — Unemployment compensation.

21-386-57 — Workers' compensation.

36-653-4 — Unemployment work relief up to $60 per month.

TOOLS OF TRADE

36-651-121 — Tools, books, uniforms, implements, instruments, furnishings, fishing boat, nets, motor vehicle and other personal property needed for livelihood.

INSURANCE

24-431:10-231 — Disability benefits.

24-431:10-232 — Annuity contract or endowment policy proceeds if beneficiary is insured spouse, child or parent.

24-431:10-233 — Group life insurance policy or proceeds.

24-431:10-234 — Life or health insurance policy for child.

24-431:10-D:112 — Life insurance proceeds if policy prohibits use to pay creditors.

24-432:2-403 — Fraternal benefit society benefits.

IDAHO

References are to Idaho Code. Example: "I.C. s.55-1201". Ignore volume number.

HOMESTEAD

55-1201 — $25,000. Sale proceeds are exempt for 6 months. Before filing for bankruptcy, you must file a homestead declaration.

PERSONAL PROPERTY

11-603 — Health aids; burial plot.

11-604 — Personal injury and wrongful death recoveries needed for support.

11-605 — Motor vehicle up to $500; jewelry up to $250; clothing, pets, appliances, furnishings, books, musical instruments, 1 firearm, family portraits and sentimental heirlooms up to $500 per item, but only up to $4,000 total; crops cultivated by the debtor on up to 50 acres (including water rights up to 160 inches) to $1,000.

11-606 — Proceeds for damaged exempt property, for up to 3 months after received.

45-514 — Building materials.

WAGES

11-207 — Minimum of 75% of earned but unpaid wages and pension payments. Judge may approve more for low income debtors.

PENSIONS

11-604 — Payments being received from pensions needed for support, provided payments are not mixed with other money.

50-1517 — Police officers.

59-1325 — Public employees.

72-1417 — Firefighters.

PUBLIC BENEFITS

11-603 — Unemployment compensation, social security, veterans' benefits, and federal, state and local public assistance.

56-223 — General assistance, AFDC, and aid to blind, aged and disabled.

TOOLS OF TRADE

11-605 — Tools, books and implements of trade up to $1,000; arms, uniforms and accoutrements required to be kept by peace officer, national guard or military personnel.

ALIMONY AND CHILD SUPPORT

11-604 — Alimony and child support needed for support.

INSURANCE

11-603 — Medical or hospital care benefits

11-604;41-1834 — Death and disability benefits.

41-1830 — Life insurance policy if the beneficiary is a married woman.

41-1833 — Life insurance proceeds, dividends, interest, loan, cash or surrender value if the insured is not the beneficiary.

41-1835 — Group life insurance benefits.

41-1836 — Annuity contract proceeds up to $350 per month.

41-1930 — Life insurance proceeds if policy prohibits use to pay creditors.

41-3218 — Fraternal benefit society benefits.

55-1201 — Homeowners's insurance proceeds up to $25,000.

ILLINOIS   References are to Illinois Statutes Annotated. Example: "I.R.S. s.110-12-901".

HOMESTEAD (**)
110-12-901	Real or personal property, including a farm, lot and buildings, condominium, coop or mobile home, up to $7,500.

PERSONAL PROPERTY
110-12-1001	Motor vehicle up to $1,200; clothing needed; health aids; school books; family pictures; bible; personal injury recoveries up to $7,500; wrongful death recoveries needed for support; proceeds from sale of exempt property; any other personal property up to $2,000 (including wages).

WAGES
110-12-803	Minimum 85% of earned but unpaid wages. Judge may approve more for low income debtor.

PENSIONS
108.5-2-154	General assembly members.
108.5-3-144.1; 108.5-5-218	Police officers.
108.5-4-135; 108.5-6-213	Firefighters.
108.5-7-217; 108.5-8-244	Municipal employees.
108.5-9-228	County employees.
108.5-11-223	Civil service employees.
108.5-12-190	Park employeeds.
108.5-13-213	Sanitation district employees.
108.5.14-147	State employees.
108.5-15-185	State university employees.
108.5-16-190; 108.5-17-151	Teachers.

108.5-18-161	Judges.
108.5-19-117	House of correction employees.
108.5-22-230	Disabled firefighters, and widows and children of firefighters..

PUBLIC BENEFITS
23-11-3	AFDC; aid to blind, aged and disabled.
48-138.21	Workers' compensation.
48-172.56	Workers' occupational disease compensation.
48-540	Unemployment compensation.
110-12-1001	Veterans' benefits; social security; crime victims' compensation.

TOOLS OF TRADE
110-12-1001	Tools, books and implements of trade up to $750.

ALIMONY AND CHILD SUPPORT
110-12-1001	Alimony and child support needed for support.

INSURANCE
73-850	Life insurance, annuity or cash value if beneficiary is spouse, child, parent, or other dependent.
73-853	Life insurance proceeds if policy prohibits use to pay creditors.
73-925	Fraternal benefit society benefits.
110-12-907	Homeowners' insurance proceeds for destroyed home, up to $7,500.
110-12-1001	Health and disability benefits, life insurance proceeds needed for support, and life insurance policy if beneficiary is spouse or child.

INDIANA   References are to Annotated Indiana Code. Example: "A.I.C. s.34-2-28-1".

HOMESTEAD
34-2-28-1	Real or personal property used as a residence up to $7,500 (LIMIT: homestead plus personal property can't exceed $10,000); tenancies by the entirety exempt without limit unless bankruptcy is seeking to discharge debts incurred by both spouses.

PERSONAL PROPERTY
34-2-28-1	Health aids; up to $4,000 of real or tangible personal property; up to $100 of intangible personal property (except for money owed to you).

WAGES
24-4.5-5-105	Minimum of 75% of earned but unpaid wages. Judge may approve more for low income debtors.

PENSIONS
5-10.3-8-9	Public employees.
10-1-2-9; 36-8-8-17	Police officers, but only as to benefits accruing.
21-6.1-5-17	State teachers.
36-8-7-22; 36-8-8-17	Firefighters.
36-8-10-19	Sheriffs, but only benefits accruing.

PUBLIC BENEFITS
16-7-3.6-15	Crime victims' compensation, unless seeking to discharge debt for treatment of crime-related injury.
22-3-2-17	Workers' compensation.
22-4-33-3	Unemployment compensation.

TOOLS OF TRADE
10-2-6-3	National guard arms, uniforms and equipment.

INSURANCE
27-1-12-14	Life insurance policy or proceeds if beneficiary is spouse or dependent.
27-1-12-29	Group life insurance policy.
27-2-5-1	Life insurance proceeds if policy prohibits use to pay creditors.
27-8-3-23	Mutual life or accident policy proceeds.
27-11-6-3	Fraternal benefit society benefits.

IOWA

References are to Iowa Code Annotated. Example: "I.C.A. s.449A.18". Ignore volume numbers; look for "section" numbers.

HOMESTEAD

499A.18; 561.2; 561.16 — Real property or apartment, unlimited in value, but cannot exceed 1/2 acre in a city or town, or 40 acres elsewhere.

PERSONAL PROPERTY

627.6 — Motor vehicle, musical instruments and tax refunds up to $5,000 total (but tax refund portion limited to $1,000 of the total); clothing up to $1,000, plus receptacles to hold clothing; household goods, appliances, and furnishings up to $2,000 total; wedding and engagement rings; books, portraits, paintings and pictures up to $1,000; health aids; burial plot up to 1 acre; rifle or musket; shotgun; up to $100 of any other personal property including cash.

WAGES

642.21 — Minimum of 75% of earned but unpaid wages and pension payments. Judge may approve more for low income debtors.

PENSIONS

97A-12 — Peace officers.
97B-39 — Public employees.
410.11 — Disabled firefighters and police officers, but only for benefits being received.
411.13 — Police officers and firefighters.
627.6 — Other pensions needed for support, but only as to payments being received, including IRAs.

627.8 — Federal government pension, but only as to payments being received.

PUBLIC BENEFITS

627.6 — Unemployment compensation, veterans' benefits, social security, and AFDC.
627.13 — Workers' compensation.
627.19 — Adopted child assistance.

TOOLS OF TRADE

627.6 — Non-farming equipment up to $10,000; farming equipment, including livestock and feed, up to $10,000; but not inlcuding a car.

ALIMONY AND CHILD SUPPORT

627.6 — Alimony and child support needed for support.

INSURANCE

508.32 — Life insurance proceeds if policy prohibits use to pay creditors.
509.12 — Employee group insurance policy or proceeds.
627.6 — Life insurance proceeds up to $10,000, (if acquired within 2 years prior to filing for bankruptcy); and accident, disability, health, illness or life proceeds, dividends, interest, loan, cash or surrender value; if beneficiary is spouse, child or other dependent.

KANSAS

References are to Kansas Statutes Annotated. Example: K.S.A. s.60-2301". Ignore volume numbers; look for "section" numbers.

HOMESTEAD

60-2301 — Real property or mobile home of unlimited value, but can't exceed 1 acre in a city or town, or 160 acres on a farm. You must occupy or intend to occupy the property at the time you file for bankruptcy. (Also refer to "Const. 15-9").

PERSONAL PROPERTY

60-2304 — Motor vehicle up to $20,000 (no limit if equipped or designed for a disabled person); clothing to last 1 year; household equipment and furnishings; food and fuel to last 1 year; jewelry and articles of adornment up to $1,000; burial plot.

WAGES

60-2310 — Minimum of 75% of earned but unpaid wages. Judge may approve more for low income debtor.

PENSIONS

12-5005; 13-14a10 — Police officers.
12-5005; 14-10a10 — Firefighters.
13-14,102 — Elected and appointed officials in cities with populations of between 120,000 and 200,000.
60-2308 — Federal government pension needed for support and received within 3 months prior to filing bankruptcy.
72-5526 — State school employees.

74-2618 — Judges.
74-4923; 74-49,105 — Public employees.
74-4989 — State highway patrol officers.

PUBLIC BENEFITS

39-717 — AFDC; general assistance; social welfare.
44-514 — Workers' compensation.
44-718 — Unemployment compensation.
74-7313 — Crime victims' compensation.

TOOLS OF TRADE

60-2304 — Equipment, instruments, furniture, books, documents, breeding stock, seed, stock and grain up to $7,500 total.

INSURANCE

40-258 — Life insurance proceeds up to $1,000, but only if payable to the decedent's estate.
40-414 — Life insurance proceeds or cash value deposited into a bank account; life insurance forfeiture value, only if policy issued over 1 year prior to filing for bankruptcy; fraternal benefit society benefits.
40-414a — Life insurance proceeds if policy prohibits use to pay creditors.

133

KENTUCKY

References are to Kentucky Revised Statutes. Example: "K.R.S. s.427.060". Ignore volume numbers; look for "chapter" numbers.

HOMESTEAD
427.060   Real or personal property used as a family residence up to $5,000. Sale proceeds are also exempt up to $1,000.

PERSONAL PROPERTY
304.39-260   Reparation benefits received and medical expenses paid under motor vehicle reparation law.

427.010   Motor vehicle up to $2,500; health aids; clothing, furniture, jewelry and articles of adornment up to $3,000 total.

427.060   Burial plot up to $5,000, in lieu of homestead.

427.150   Lost earnings payments needed for support; wrongful death recoveries for person you depended upon for support; personal injury recoveries up to $7,500, but not including pain, suffering or pecuniary loss.

427.160 $1,000 of any other property.

WAGES
427.101   Minimum of 75% of earned but unpaid wages. Judge may approve more for low income debtor.

PENSIONS
61.690   State employees.

67A.350   Urban county government employees.

67A.620;95.878;
427.120;427.125   Police officers and firefighters.

161.700   Teachers.

427.150   Other pensions needed for support, including IRAs.

PUBLIC BENEFITS
205.220   AFDC; aid to blind, aged and disabled.

341.470   Unemployment compensation.

342.180   Workers' compensation.

427.150   Crime victims' compensation.

TOOLS OF TRADE
427.010   Farmer's tools, equipment, livestock and poultry up to $3,000.

427.030   Non-farmer's tools up to $300; motor vehicle of mechanic, mechanical or electrical equipment servicer, minister, attorney, physician, surgeon, dentist, veterinarian or chiropractor up to $2,500.

427.040   Library, office equipment, instruments and furnishings of a minister, attorney, physician, surgeon, dentist, veterinarian or chiropractor up to $1,000.

ALIMONY AND CHILD SUPPORT
427.150   Alimony and child support needed for support.

INSURANCE
304.14-300   Life insurance proceeds or cash value if beneficiary is not the insured.

304.14-310   Health or disability benefits.

304.14-320   Group life insurance proceeds.

304.14-330   Annuity contract proceeds up to $350 per month.

304.14-340   Life insurance policy if the beneficiary is a married woman.

304.14-350   Life insurance proceeds if policy prohibits use to pay creditors.

LOUISIANA

References are to Louisiana Revised Statutes Annotated. Example: "L.R.S.A. s.20:1". Ignore volume numbers; look for "section" numbers. Also, be sure to use the volumes marked "Revised Statutes".

HOMESTEAD
20:1   Up to $15,000, but cannot exceed 160 acres on one tract, or 160 acres on more than 1 tract if there is only a home on one of the tracts. Must occupy at time of filing bankruptcy. Spouse or child of deceased owner, or spouse obtaining home in divorce, may claim exemption.(**)

PERSONAL PROPERTY
8:313   Cemetary plot and monuments.

13:3881   Living room, dining room and bedroom furniture; clothing; chinaware, glassware, utensils, and silverware (but not sterling); refrigerator, freezer, stove, washer and dryer; bedding and linens; family portraits; musical instruments; heating and cooling equipment; pressing irons and sewing machine; arms and military accoutrements; poultry, fowl and 1 cow; engagement and wedding rings up to $5,000; and equipment needed for therapy.

WAGES
13:3881   Minimum of 75% of earned but unpaid wages. Judge may approve more for low income debtor.

PUBLIC BENEFITS
23:1205   Workers' compensation.

23:1693   Unemployment compensation.

46:111   AFDC; aid to blind, aged and disabled.

46:1811   Crime victims' compensation.

TOOLS OF TRADE
13:3881   Tools, books, instruments, non-luxury car, pickup truck (up to 3 tons), and utility trailer needed for work.

INSURANCE
22:558   Fraternal benefit society benefits.

22:646   Health, accident or disability proceeds, dividends, interest, loan, cash or surrender value.

22:647   Life insurance proceeds, dividends, interest, loan, cash or surrender value.

22:649   Group insurance policies or proceeds.

MAINE References are to Maine Revised Statutes Annotated. Example: "M.R.S.A. s.14-4422". Ignore volume numbers; look for "title" numbers.

HOMESTEAD
14-4422	$7,500.(**)

PERSONAL PROPERTY
9-A-5-103	Balance due on repossessed goods, provided total amount financed is not more than $2,000.
14-4422	Motor vehicle up to $1,200; cooking stove; furnaces and stoves for heat; food to last 6 months; fuel not to exceed 5 tons of coal, 1,000 gallons of oil, or 10 cords of wood; health aids; wedding and engagement rings; other jewelry up to $500; lost earnings payments needed for support; feed, seed, fertilizer, tools and equipment to raise and harvest food for 1 season; wrongful death recoveries needed for support; personal injury recoveries up to $7,500, not including pain and suffering.
14-4422	Clothing, household goods and furnishings, appliances, tools of trade (in addition to exemption listed below), and personal injury recoveries (in addition to exemption listed below) up to a total of $4,500, but only in lieu of homestead exemption.
14-4422	Burial plot up to $7,500, in lieu of homestead exemption.
37-B-262	Military arms, clothes and equipment.

WAGES:
None

PENSIONS
3-703	Legislators.
4-1203	Judges.
5-17054	State employees.

PUBLIC BENEFITS
14-4422	Unemployment compensation, veterans' benefits, social security, and crime victims' compensation.
22-3753	AFDC
39-67	Workers' compensation.

TOOLS OF TRADE
14-4422	Books, materials and stock up to $1,000; 1 of each type of farm implement necessary to raise and harvest crops; 1 boat not to exceed 5 tons used in commercial fishing.

ALIMONY AND CHILD SUPPORT
14-4422	Alimony and child support needed for support.

INSURANCE
14-4422	Unmatured life insurance policy; life insurance policy, dividends, interest, or loan value for person you depended upon up to $4,000.
24-A-2428	Life, annuity, accident or endowment policy, proceeds, dividends, interest, loan, cash or surrender value.
24-A-2429	Disability or health insurance proceeds, dividends, interest, loan, cash or surrender value.
24-A-2430	Group life or health policy or proceeds.
24-A-2431	Annuity proceeds up to $450 per month.
24-A-4118	Fraternal benefit society benefits.

MARYLAND References of numbers only are to Annotated Code of Maryland. Example: "A.C.M. s.23-164". Other references are to specific subject volumes. Look for the title of these. Example: A.C.M. Courts and Judicial Procedure s.11-504.

HOMESTEAD:
None.

PERSONAL PROPERTY
Ct.&Jud.Proc.11-504	Clothing, household goods, appliances, furnishings, books and pets up to $500 total; health aids; cash up to $3,000; lost future earnings recoveries; $2,500 of any property.
23-164	Burial plot.

WAGES
Comm.15-601.1	Earned but unpaid wages are exempt as follows: in Kent, Caroline and Queen Anne's of Worcester counties, the greater of 75% of actual wages or 30% of the federal minimum wage; in all other counties, the greater of 75% or $145 per week.

PENSIONS
73B-17;73B-125	State employees.
73B-49	Deceased Baltimore police officers, but only as to benefits accruing.
73B-96;73B-152	Teachers.
88B-60	State police.

PUBLIC BENEFITS
26A-13	Crime victims' compensation.
88A-73	AFDC; general assistance.
95A-16	Unemployment compensation.
101-50	Workers' compensation.

TOOLS OF TRADE
Ct.&Jud.Proc.11-504	Tools, books, instruments, appliances and clothing needed for work (but can't include car).

INSURANCE
48A-328,Estates and Trusts 8-115	Fraternal benefit society benefits.
48A-385,Estates and Trusts 8-115	Life insurance or annuity contract proceeds, dividends, interest, loan, cash or surrender value if beneficiary is a dependent of the insured.
Comm.15-601.1	Medical benefits deducted from wages.
Ct.&Jud.Proc.11-504	Disability or health benefits.

HOMESTEAD

188-1;188-1A	$1,000,000; if over 65 or disabled then $150,000. Some tenancies by the entirety are exempt without limit. Must record homestead declaration before filing bankruptcy. Must occupy or intend to occupy the property at the time of filing for bankruptcy. Spouse or child of deceased owner may claim the exemption.(*)

PERSONAL PROPERTY

79-6A	Moving expenses for eminent domain (that is, if the government took your property).
235-34	Motor vehicle up to $700; furniture up to $3,000; clothing needed; beds and bedding; heating unit; books up to $200 total; cash up to $200 per month for rent, in lieu of homestead; cash for fuel, heat, water or electricity up to $75 per month; bank deposits to $125; cash for food or food to $300; sewing machine to $200; burial plots and tombs; church pew; 2 cows, 2 swine, 12 sheep and 4 tons of hay.
246-28A	Bank, credit union or trust company deposits up to $500 total.

WAGES

246-28	Earned but unpaid wages up to $125 per week; payments being received up to $100 per week.

PENSIONS

32-19	Public employees.
32-41	Private retirement benefits.
168-41	Savings bank employees.

PUBLIC BENEFITS.

115-5	Veterans' benefits.
118-10	AFDC
151A-36	Unemployment compensation.
152-47	Workers' compensation.
235-34	Aid to aged and disabled.

TOOLS OF TRADE

235-34	Tools, implements and fixtures up to $500 total; materials you designed and procured up to $500; boats, nets and fishing tackle of fisherman up to $500; arms, uniforms and accoutrements you are required to keep.

INSURANCE

175-110A	Disability benefits up to $35 per week.
175-119A	Life insurance proceeds if policy prohibits use to pay creditors.
175-125	Life insurance annuity contract which states it is exempt; life or endowment policy, proceeds, dividends, interest, loan, cash or surrender value.
175-126	Life insurance policy if beneficiary is a married woman.
175-132C	Group annuity policy or proceeds.
175-135	Group life insurance policy.
175F-15	Medical malpractice self-insurance.
176-22	Fraternal benefit society benefits.

HOMESTEAD

559.214; 600.6023; 600.6027	Real property, including condominium, up to $3,500; but not to exceed 1 lot in a city, town or village, or 40 acres elsewhere. Some tenancies by the entirety are exempt without limit. Spouse or child of a deceased owner may claim the exemption.

PERSONAL PROPERTY

128.112	Burial plots.
600.6023	Clothing; household goods, furniture, appliances, utensils and books up to $1,000 total; food and fuel to last 6 months if head of household; building and loan association shares up to $1,000 par value, in lieu of homestead exemption; family pictures; church pew, slip or seat; 2 cows, 5 swine, 10 sheep, 5 roosters, 100 hens, and hay and grain to last 6 months if head of household.

WAGES

600.5311	60% of earned but unpaid wages for head of household; 40% for others; suject to following minimums: $15 per week plus $2 per week for each dependent other than spouse for head of household; $10 per week for others.

PENSIONS

38.40	State employees.
38.559	Police officers and firefighters.
38.826	Judges.
38.927	Probate judges.
38.1057	Legislators.
38.1346	Public school employees.
600.6023	IRAs, to extent tax-deferred.

PUBLIC BENEFITS

35.926	Veterans' benefits for WWII veterans.
35.977	Korean War veterans' benefits.
35.1027	Vietnam veterans' benefits.
330.1158a	AFDC
400.63	Social welfare benefits.
418.821	Workers' compensation.
421.30	Unemployment compensation.

TOOLS OF TRADE

600.6023	Tools, implements, materials, stock, apparatus, motor vehicle, horse, team and harness up to $1,000 total; arms and accoutrements you are required to keep.

INSURANCE

500.2207	Life insurance proceeds, dividends, interest, loan, cash or surrender value; life or endowment proceeds if beneficiary is spouse or child of insured.
500.2209	Life insurance proceeds up to $300 per year if the beneficiary is a married woman or a husband.
500.4054	Life, annuity or endowment proceeds if policy or contract prohibits use to pay creditors.
500.8046	Fraternal benefit society benefits.
600.6023	Disability, mutual life or health benefits.

MINNESOTA References are to Minnesota Statutes Annotated. Example: "M.S.A. s.510.01." Ignore volume numbers; look for "section" numbers.

HOMESTEAD

510.01;510.02; 550.37	Real property, mobile or manufacturer home of unlimited value, but cannot exceed 1/2 acre in a city or 160 acres elsewhere.

PERSONAL PROPERTY

550.37	Motor vehicle up to $2,000; clothing, including watch; furniture, appliances, radio, TV and phonographs up to $4,500 total; food and utensils; books; burial plot; church pew or seat; proceeds for damaged exempt property; personal injury lost earnings and wrongful death recoveries.

WAGES

550.37	Wages deposited into bank accounts for 20 days after deposit; earned but unpaid wages paid within 6 months of returning to work if you previously received welfare; wages of released inmates paid received within 6 months of release.
571.55	Minimum of 75% of earned but unpaid wages. Judge may approve more for low income debtor.

PENSIONS

181B.16	Private retirement benefits accruing.
352.15	State employees.
352B.071	State troopers.
353.15	Public employees.
354.10;354A.11	Teachers.

PUBLIC BENEFITS

176.175	Workers' compensation.
268.17	Unemployment compensation.
550.37	AFDC, supplemental security income (SSI), general assistance, supplemental assistance.
550.38	Veterans' benefits.
611A.60	Crime victims' compensation.

TOOLS OF TRADE

550.37	Tools, library, furniture, machines, instruments, implements and stock in trade up to $5,000; Farm machines, implements, livestock, produce and crops of farmers up to $10,000. (Total of these cannot exceed $10,000.) Teaching materials of a school teacher, including books and chemical apparatus, of unlimited value and not subject to $10,000 limit.

INSURANCE

61A.04	Life insurance proceeds if policy prohibits use to pay creditors.
61A.12	Life insurance or endowment proceeds, dividends, interest, loan, cash or surrender value if the insured is not the beneficiary.
64B.18	Fraternal benefit society benefits.
550.37	Life insurance proceeds if beneficiary is spouse or child, up to $20,000 plus additional $5,000 per dependent; unmatured life insurance contract dividends, interest, loan, cash or surrender value if insured is the debtor or someone the debtor depends upon, up to $4,000; police, fire or beneficiary association benefits.
550.39	Accident or disability proceeds.

MISCELLANEOUS

550.37	Earnings of a minor child.

MISSISSIPPI References are to Mississippi Code. Example: "M.C. s.85-3-21".

HOMESTEAD

85-3-21	$30,000, but cannot exceed 160 acres. Must occupy at time of filing bankruptcy, unless you are widowed or over 60 and married. Sale proceeds are also exempt.

PERSONAL PROPERTY

85-3-1	Tangible personal property of any kind up to $10,000; proceeds from exempt property.

WAGES

85-3-4	Earned but unpaid wages owed for 30 days, 75% after 30 days.

PENSIONS

21-29-257	Police officers and firefighters.
25-11-129	Public employees retirement and disability benefits.
25-11-201-23	Teachers.
25-13-31	Highway patrol officers.
25-14-5	State employees.
71-1-43	Private retirement benefits.

PUBLIC BENEFITS

25-11-129	Social security.
43-3-71	Assistance to blind.
43-9-19	Assistance to aged.
43-29-15	Assistance to disabled.
71-3-43	Workers' compensation.
71-5-539	Unemployment compensation.

TOOLS OF TRADE: None.

INSURANCE

83-7-5	Life insurance proceeds if policy prohibits use to pay creditors.
83-29-39	Fraternal benefit society benefits.
85-3-1	Disability benefits.
85-3-11	Life insurance policy or proceeds up to $50,000.
85-3-13	Life insurance proceeds if beneficiary is the decedent's estate, up to $5,000.
85-3-23	Homeowners' insurance proceeds up to $30,000.

137

MISSOURI References are to Annotated Missouri Statutes. Example: "A.M.S. s.513.430". Ignore volume numbers; look for "section" numbers..

HOMESTEAD
513.430;513.475	Real property up to $8,000, or mobile home up to $1,000. Some tenancies by the entirety are exempt without limit.(*)

PERSONAL PROPERTY
214.190	Burial grounds up to $100 or 1 acre.
513.430	Motor vehicle up to $500; clothing, household goods, appliances, furnishings, books, animals, musical instruments and crops up to $1,000 total; health aids; jewelry up to $500; wrongful death recoveries for a person you depended upon.
513.430;513.440	Any property up to $1,250 plus $250 per child for head of family; up to $400 for others.
Other	Personal injury causes of action. Refer to as: "In re Mitchell, 73 B.R. 93".

WAGES
513.470	Wages of a servant or common laborer up to $90.
525.030	Minimum of 75% of earned but unpaid wages. Judge may approve more for low income debtor.

PENSIONS
70.695	Public officers and employees.
71.207	Employees of cities with more than 100,000 population.
86.190;86.353; 86.493;86.780 87.090;87.365;	Police department employees.
87.485	Firefighters.
104.250	Highway and transportation employees.
104.540	State employees.
169.090	Teachers.

PUBLIC BENEFITS
287.260	Workers' compensation.
288.380;513.430	Unemployment compensation.
513.430	Social security, veterans' benefits, and AFDC.

TOOLS OF TRADE
513.430	Tools, books and implements to $2,000.

ALIMONY AND CHILD SUPPORT
513.430	Alimony and child support up to $500 per month.

INSURANCE
376.530;376.560	Life insurance proceeds if policy owned by woman insuring her husband.
376.550	Life insurance proceeds if policy owned by an unmarried woman and beneficiary is her father or brother.
377.090	Fraternal benefit society benefits.
377.330	Assessment or stipulated premium proceeds.
513.430	Death, disability or illness benefits needed for support; unmatured life insurance policy.

MONTANA References are to Montana Code Annotated. Example: "M.C.A. s.70-32-101". Ignore volume numbers; look for "title" numbers.

HOMESTEAD
70-32-101; 70-32-104	Real property or mobile home up to $40,000. Must occupy at time of filing for bankruptcy, and must record a homestead declaration before filing.

PERSONAL PROPERTY
25-13-608	Health aids; burial plot.
25-13-609	Motor vehicle up to $1,200; clothing, household goods and furnishings, appliances, jewelry, books, animals and feed, musical instruments, firearms, sporting goods, and crops up to $600 per item and $4,500 total.
25-13-610	Proceeds for damaged or lost exempt property for 6 months after receipt.
35-15-404	Cooperative association shares up to $500 value.

WAGES
25-13-614	Minimum of 75% of earned but unpaid wages. Judge may approve more for low income debtor.

PENSIONS
19-3-105	Public employees.
19-4-706	Teachers.
19-5-704	Judges.
19-6-705	Highway patrol officers.
19-7-705	Sheriffs.
19-8-805	Game wardens.
19-9-1006; 19-10-504	Police officers.
19-11-612; 19-13-1004	Firefighters.

PUBLIC BENEFITS
25-13-608	Social security and veterans' benefits.
39-71-743	Workers' compensation.
39-73-110	Silicosis benefits.
39-51-3105	Unemployment compensation.
53-2-607	AFDC, aid to aged and disabled, vocational rehabilitation to the blind, subsidized adoption payments.
53-9-129	Crime victims' compensation.

TOOLS OF TRADE
25-13-609	Tools, books and instruments of trade up to $3,000.
25-13-613	Arms, uniforms and accoutrements needed to carry out government functions.

ALIMONY AND CHILD SUPPORT
25-13-608	Alimony and child support.

INSURANCE
25-13-608; 33-15-513	Disability or illness proceeds, benefits, dividends, interest, loan, cash or surrender value, and medical or hospital benefits.
25-13-609	Unmatured life insurance contracts up to $4,000.
33-7-511	Fraternal benefit society benefits.
33-15-511	Life insurance proceeds, dividends, interest, loan, cash or surrender value.
33-15-512	Group life insurance policy or proceeds.
33-15-514	Annuity contract proceeds up to $350 per month.
33-20-120	Life insurance proceeds if policy prohibits use to pay creditors.
80-2-245	Hail insurance benefits.

NEBRASKA   References are to Revised Statutes of Nebraska. Example: "R.S.N. s.40-101". Ignore volume numbers; look for "chapter" numbers.

HOMESTEAD
40-101 $10,000, but cannot exceed 2 lots in a city or 160 acres elsewhere. Sale proceeds are exempt for 6 months after sale.

PERSONAL PROPERTY
12-511   Perpetual care funds.
12-517   Burial plot.
12-605   Tombs, crypts, lots, niches and vaults.
25-1552 $2,500 of any property except wages, in lieu of homestead.
25-1556   Personal possessions; clothing needed; furniture and kitchen utensils up to $1,500; food and fuel to last 6 months.

WAGES
25-1558   Minimum of 85% of earned but unpaid wages or pension payments for head of family; 75% for others. Judge may approve more for low income debtor.

PENSIONS.
23-2322   County employees.
25-1559   Military disability benefits up to $2,000.
79-1060;
79-1552   School employees.
84-1324   State employees.

PUBLIC BENEFITS
48-149   Workers' compensation.
48-647   Unemployment compensation.
68-1013   AFDC; aid to blind, aged and disabled.

TOOLS OF TRADE
25-1556   Tools or equipment up to $1,500. (**)

INSURANCE
44-371   Life insurance or annuity contract proceeds up to $10,000 loan value.
44-754   Disability benefits to $200 per month.
44-1089   Fraternal benefit society benefits up to loan value of $10,000.

NEVADA   References are to Nevada Revised Statutes Annotated. Example: "N.R.S.A. s.21.090(m)". Ignore volume numbers; look for "chapter" numbers.

HOMESTEAD
21.090(m);115.010   Real property or mobile home up to $90,000. Must record a homestead declaration before filing for bankruptcy.(*)

PERSONAL PROPERTY
21.090   Motor vehicle up to $1,000; household goods, furniture, home and yard equipment up to $3,000 total; books up to $1,500 total; pictures and keepsakes.
21.100   Metal-bearing ores, geological specimens, paleontological remains or art curiosities.
452.550   Burial plot purchase money held in trust.
689.700   Funeral service contract money held in trust.

WAGES
21.090   Minimum of 75% of earned but unpaid wages. Judge may approve more for low income debtor.

PENSIONS
286.670   Public employees.

PUBLIC BENEFITS
422.291   AFDC; aid to blind, aged and disabled.
612.710   Unemployment compensation.
615.270   Vocational rehabilitation benefits.
616.550   Industrial insurance (worker's compensation).

TOOLS OF TRADE
21.090   Tools, materials, library, equipment and supplies up to $4,500; farm trucks, equipment, tools, stock and seed up to $4,500; cabin or dwelling of a miner or prospector, cars, implements and appliances for mining and a mining claim you work up to $4,500; arms, uniforms and accoutrements you are required to keep.

INSURANCE
21.090   Life insurance policy or proceeds if premiums don't exceed $1,000 per year.
687B.260   Life insurance proceeds if you are not insured.
687B.270   Health insurance proceeds, dividends, interest, loan, cash or surrender value.
687B.280   Group life or health policy or proceeds.
687B.290   Annuity contract proceeds up to $350 per month.
695A.220   Fraternal benefit society benefits.

NEW HAMPSHIRE   References are to New Hampshire Revised Statutes Annotated. Example: "N.H.R.S.A. s.480:1". Ignore volume numbers; look for "chapter" numbers..

HOMESTEAD
480:1	Real property, or manufactured home if you own the land, up to $5,000.

PERSONAL PROPERTY
511:2	Automobile up to $1,000; clothing, beds, bedsteads, bedding and cooking utensils; furniture up to $2,000; refrigerator, cooking and heating stoves; food and fuel up to $400; jewelry up to $500; books up to $800; sewing machine; burial plot, lot, and church pew; 1 cow, 6 sheep or fleece, 4 tons of hay, and 1 hog, pig or pork if already slaughtered.
512:21	Proceeds for lost or destroyed exempt property; jury and witness fee; wages of a minor child.

WAGES
512:21	Earned but unpaid wages of debtor and spouse. Judge determines amount exempt based on percent of federal mimimun wage, so claim all.

PENSIONS
100A:26	Public employees.
102:23	Firefighters.
103:18	Police officers.
512:21	Federally created pensions accruing.

PUBLIC BENEFITS
167:25	AFDC; aid to blind, aged and disabled.
282A:159	Unemployment compensation.

TOOLS OF TRADE
511:2	Tools of trade up to $1,200; arms, uniforms and equipment of a military member; 1 yoke of oxen or horse needed for farming or teaming.

ALIMONY AND CHILD SUPPORT
161C:11	Child support only.

INSURANCE
402:69	Firefighters' aid insurance.
408:1	Life insurance or endowment proceeds if beneficiary is a married woman.
408:2	Life insurance or endowment proceeds if you are not the insured.
418:24	Fraternal benefit society benefits.
512:21	Homeowners' insurance proceeds up to $5,000.

NEW JERSEY References are to New Jersey Statutes Annotated. Example: "N.J.S.A. s.2A:17-19".

PERSONAL PROPERTY
2A:17-19	Clothing; goods, personal property and stock or interest in corporations up to $1,000 total.
2A:26-4	Household good and furniture up to $1,000.
8A:5-10	Burial plots.

WAGES
2A:17-56	90% of earned but unpaid wages if your income is less than $7,500; otherwise judge may exempt less.
38A:4-8	Military personnel wages and allowances.

PENSIONS
A:057.6	Civil defense workers.
18A:66-51	Teachers.
18A:66-116	School district employees.
43:6A-41	Judges.
43:7-13	Prison employees.
43:8A-20	Alcohol beverage control officers.
43:10-57;	
43:10-105	County employees.
43:13-44	Municipal employees.
43:15A-55	Public employees.
43:16-7;	
43:16A-17	Police officers, firefighters and traffic officers.
43:18-12	City boards of health employees.
43:19-17	Street and water department employees.
53:5A-45	State police.

PUBLIC BENEFITS
34:15-29	Workers' compensation.
43:21-53	Unemployment compensation.
44:7-35	Old-age, permanent disability assistance.
52:4B-30	Crime victims' compensation.

INSURANCE
A:9-57.6	Civil defense workers' disability, death, medical or hospital benefits.
17:18-12;	
17B:24-8	Health and disability benefits.
17:44A-19	Fraternal benefit society benefits.
17B:24-6	Life insurance proceeds, dividends, interest, loan, cash or surrender value, if you are not the insured.
17B:24-7	Annuity contract proceeds up to $500 per month.
17B:24-9	Group life or health policy or proceeds.
17B:24-10	Life insurance proceeds if policy prohibits use to pay creditors.
38A:4-8	Military member disability or death benefits.

NEW MEXICO References are to New Mexico Statutes Annotated. Example: "N.M.S.A. s.42-10-9". Ignore volume numbers; look for "chapter" numbers.

HOMESTEAD
42-10-9	$20,000 only if married, widowed or supporting another person.(**)

PERSONAL PROPERTY
42-10-1	Motor vehicle up to $4,000; $500 of any property.
42-10-1;	
42-10-2	Clothing; jewelry up to $2,500; books, furniture, and health equipment.
42-10-10	$2,000 of any property, in lieu of homestead.
48-2-15	Building materials.
53-4-28	Minimum amount of shares needed for membership in cooperative association.
70-4-12	Tools, machinery and materials needed to dig, drill, torpedo, complete, operate or repair an oil line, gas well or pipeline.

WAGES
35-12-7	Minimum of 75% of earned but unpaid wages. Judge may approve more for low income debtor.

PENSIONS
22-11-42	Public school employees.
42-10-1;	
42-10-2	Pension or retirement benefits.

PUBLIC BENEFITS
27-2-21	AFDC; general assistance.
31-22-15	Crime victims' compensation paid before July 1, 1979.
51-1-37	Unemployment compensation.
52-1-52	Workers' compensation.
52-3-37	Occupational disease disablement benefits.

TOOLS OF TRADE
42-10-1;	
42-10-2	$1,500.

INSURANCE
42-10-3	Life, accident, health or annuity benefits or cash value, if beneficiary is a citizen of New Mexico.
42-10-4	Benevolent association benefits up to $5,000.
42-10-5	Life insurance proceeds.
59A-44-18	Fraternal benefit society benefits.

NEW YORK References of numbers only are to Consolidated Laws of New York, Civil Practice Law and Rules. Example: "C.P.L.R. s.5206". Other references are to "Debtor & Creditor" (D&C); "Estates, Powers & Trusts" (Est, Pow&Tr.); and "Insurance" (Insur.).

HOMESTEAD
5206	Real property, including mobile home, condominium or coop, up to $10,000.(**)

PERSONAL PROPERTY
5205	Clothing, furniture, refrigerator, TV, radio, sewing machine, security deposits with landlord or utility company, tableware, cooking utensils and crockery, stoves with food and fuel to last 60 days, health aids (including animals with food), church pew or seat, wedding ring, bible, schoolbooks, and pictures; books up to $50; burial plot without a structure up to 1/4 acre; domestic animals with food up to $450; watch up to $35; trust fund principal; 90% of trust fund income.
D&C282	Motor vehicle up to $2,400; lost earnings recoveries needed for support; personal injury recoveries up to $7,500, not including pain and suffering; wrongful death recoveries for a person you depended upon for support.
D&C283	IN LIEU OF HOMESTEAD: Cash in the lesser amount of $2,500, or an amount when added to an annuity equals $5,000.

WAGES
5205	90% of earned but unpaid wages received within 60 days of filing for bankruptcy; 90% of earnings from milk sales to milk dealers; 100% for a few militia members.

PUBLIC BENEFITS
D&C282	Unemployment benefits; veterans' benefits; social security; AFDC; aid to blind, aged and disabled; crime victims' compensation; home relief.

TOOLS OF TRADE
5205	Professional furniture, books, instruments, farm machinery, team and food for 60 days, up to $600 total; arms, swords, uniforms, equipment, horse, emblem and medal of a military member.

ALIMONY AND CHILD SUPPORT
D&C282	Alimony and child support needed for support.

INSURANCE
5205	Insurance proceeds for damaged exempt property.
5205; D&C282	Annuity contract benefits up to $5,000, if purchased within 6 months or filing for bankruptcy and not tax-deferred.
Est,Pow&Tr.7-1.5	Life insurance proceeds if policy prohibits use to pay creditors.
Insur.3212	Fraternal benefit society benefits; disability or illness benefits up to $400 per month; life insurance proceeds, dividends, interest, loan, cash or surrender value if beneficiary is not the insured.

NORTH CAROLINA References are to General Statutes of North Carolina. Example: "G.S.N.C. s.1C-1601". Ignore volume numbers; look for "chapter" numbers. For example, the homestead exemption is found in Chapter 1C, which is found in Volume 1A, Part II.

HOMESTEAD
1C-1601   Real or personal property used as a residence, including coop, up to $7,500. Some tenancies by the entirety exempt without limit. Up to $2,500 of unused portion may be applied to any property.

PERSONAL PROPERTY
1C-1601   Motor vehicle up to $1,000; health aids; clothing, household goods, furnishings, appliances, books, animals, musical instruments and crops up to $2,500 total, plus addtional $500 per dependent up to 4 dependents; personal injury and wrongful death recoveries for a person you depended uponL; $2,500 of any property, less any amount claimed for homestead or burial plot.
1C-1601   IN LIEU OF HOMESTEAD: burial plot up to $7,500.

WAGES
1-362   Earned but unpaid wages received 60 days before filing for bankruptcy.

PENSIONS
118-49   Firefighters and resue squad workers.
120-4.29   Legislators.
128-31   Munaicipal, city and county employees.
135-9;135-95   Teachers and state employees.
143-166.30   Law enforcement officers.

PUBLIC BENEFITS
96-17   Unemployment compensation.
97-21   Workers' compensation.
108A-36   AFDC; special adult assistance.
111-18   Aid to blind.

TOOLS OF TRADE
1C-1601   Tools, books and implements of trade up to $500.

INSURANCE
Const.10-5   Life insurance policy if beneficiary is insured spouse or child.
58-206   Life insurance proceeds, dividends, interest, loan, cash or surrender value.
58-213   Group life insurance policy or proceeds.
58-340.18   Fraternal benefit society benefits.

NORTH DAKOTA References are to North Dakota Century Code. Example: "N.D.C.C. s.28-22-02". Ignore volume numbers; look for "title" numbers.

HOMESTEAD
28-22-02;
47-18-01   Real property, mobile home or house trailer up to $80,000.

PERSONAL PROPERTY
The following list applies to all debtors:
28-22-02   Clothing; fuel to last 1 year; bible; books up to $100; pictures; church pew; burial plots; crops or grain raised on the debtor's tract of land, limited to 1 tract of 160 acres.
28-22-03.1   Motor vehicle up to $1,200; personal injury recoveries not including pain and suffering, up to $7,500; wrongful death recoveries up to $7,500.
28-22-03.1   IN LIEU OF HOMESTEAD: cash to $7,500.

The following list applies to the head of household, not claiming crops or grain:
28-22-03 $5,000 of any personal property; OR
28-22-04   Furniture and bedding up to $1,000; books and musical instruments up to $1,500; tools and library of a professional up to $1,000; tools of a mechanic and stock in trade up to $1,000; and farm implements and livestock up to $4,500.

The following list applied to a non-head of household not claiming crops:
28-22-05 $2,500 of anby personal property.

WAGES
32-09.1-.03   Minimum of 75f% of earned but unpaid wages. Judge may apporve more for low income debtor.

PENSIONS
28-22-03.1   Disabled veterans' benefits (does not include military retirement pay); annuities, pensions, IRAs, Keoghs, simplified employee plans (together with the insurance exemption under this section total may not exceed $200,000, although no limit if needed for support).
28-22-19   Public employees.
54-52-12   State employees.

PUBLIC BENEFITS
28-22-03.1   Social security.
28-22-19   AFDC; crime victims' compensation.
37-25-07   Vietnam veterans' adjustment compensation.
52-06-30   Unemployment compensation.
65-05-29   Workers' compensation.

TOOLS OF TRADE:See personal property section.

INSURANCE
26.1-15.1-18;
  26.1-33-40   Fraternal benefit society benefits.
26.1-33-40   Life insurance proceeds payable to the decedent's estate.
28-22-03.1   Life insurance surrender value up to $100,000 per policy if beneficiary is relative of the insured and the policy was owned for more than 1 year before filing for bankruptcy. Together with pension exemption in this section total cannot exceed $200,000, although no limit if needed for support.

OHIO
References are to Ohio Revised Code. Example: "O.R.C. s.2329.66".

HOMESTEAD

2329.66	Real or personal property used as a residence up to $5,000. Some tenancies by the entirety are exempt without limit.

PERSONAL PROPERTY

517.09;2329.66	Burial plot.
2329.66	Motor vehicle up to $1,000; one piece of juewelry up to $400; household goods, furnishings, appliances, jewelry, books, animals, musical instruments, firearms, hunting and fishing equipment and crops up to $200 per item, $1,500 total (IN LIEU OF HOMESTEAD: $2,000 total); clothing, beds and bedding up to $200 per item; cooking unit and refrigerator up to $300 each; health aids; lost future earnings needed for support; cash, bank and security deposits, tax refund and money due within 90 days up to $400 total; personal injury recoveries not including pain and suffering up to $5,000; wrongful death recoveries for person you depended upon for support; $400 of any property.

WAGES

2329.66	Minimum of 75% of earned but unpaid wages. Judge may approve more for low income debtor.

PENSIONS

145.56	Public employees.
146.13	Volunteer firefighters' dependents.
742.47	Police officers and firefighters.
2329.66	Police officers' and firefighters' death benefits; IRAs and Keoghs needed for support.
3307.71;3309.66	Public school employees.
5505.22	State highway patrol employees.

PUBLIC BENEFITS

2329.66;4123.67	Workers' compensation.
2329.66;4141.32	Unemployment compensation.
2329.66;5107.12	AFDC
2743.66	Crime victims' compensation.
3304.19	Vocational rehabilitation benefits.

TOOLS OF TRADE

147.04	Seal and official register of a notary public.
2329.66	Tools, books and implements of trade up to $750.

ALIMONY AND CHILD SUPPORT

2329.66	Alimony and child support needed for support.

INSURANCE

2329.63;2329.66	Benevolent society benefits to $5,000.
2329.66;3917.05	Group life insurance policy or proceeds.
2329.66;3921.18	Fraternal benefit society benefits.
2329.66;3923.19	Disability benefits to $600 per month.
3911.10	Life, endowment or annuity contract dividends, interest, loan, cash or surrender value for your spouse, child or other dependent.
3911.12	Life insurance proceeds for spouse.
3911.14	Life insurance proceeds if policy prohibits use to pay creditors.

OKLAHOMA
References are to Oklahoma Statutes Annotated. Example: "O.S.A. s.31-2".

HOMESTEAD

31-2	Real property or manufactured home to unlimited value, but cannot exceed 1/4 acre. If over 1/4 acre, you may claim up to $5,000 on 1 acre in a city, town or village, or $5,000 on 160 acres elsewhere. You do not need to occupy the home as long as you don't acquire another.

PERSONAL PROPERTY

8-7	Burial plots.
31-1	Motor vehicle up to $3,000; clothing up to $4,000; furniture, books, portraits, pictures, gun and health aids; food to last 1 year; 2 bridles and 2 saddles; 100 chickens, 20 sheep, 10 hogs, 5 cows and calves under 6 months, 2 horses and forage for livestock to last 1 year; personal injury, workers'compensation and wrongful death recoveries (not to include punitive damages) up to $50,000 total.

WAGES

12-1171.1;31-1	75% of wages earned within 90 days prior to filing bankruptcy. Judge may approve more if you can show hardship.

PENSIONS

11-49-126	Firefighters.
11-50-124	Police officers.
19-959	County employees.
31-7	Disabled vererans.
47-2-303.3	Law enforcement employees.
60-328	Tax exempt benefits.
70-17-109	Teachers.

PUBLIC BENEFITS

21-142.13	Crime victims' compensation.
40-2-303	Unemployment compensation.
56-173	AFDC; social security.
85-48	Workers' compensation.

TOOLS OF TRADE

31-1	Tools, books, apparatus of trade, and husbandry implements to farm homestead, up to $5,000 total.

ALIMONY AND CHILD SUPPORT

31-1	Alimony and child support.

INSURANCE

36-2410	Assessment or mutual benefits.
36-2510	Limited stock insurance benefits.
36-2720	Fraternal benefit society benefits.
36-3631	Life insurance policy or proceeds if you are not the insured.
36-3632	Group life insurance policy or proceeds if you are not the insured.
36-6125	Funeral benefits if pre-paid and placed in trust.

OREGON   References are to Oregon Revised Statutes. Example: "O.R.S. s.23.164". Ignore volume numbers; look for "chapter" numbers.

HOMESTEAD

23.164;23.250   Real property, houseboat, or mobile home on land you own up to $15,000 ($20,000 if joint owners). For mobile home on land you don't own, $13,000 ($18,000 if joint owners). Property may not exceed 1 block in a city or town, or 160 acres elsewhere. Must occupy or intend to occupy at time of filing for bankruptcy. Sale proceeds are exempt 1 year from sale if you plan to purchase another home.

PERSONAL PROPERTY

23.160   Motor vehicle up to $1,200(**); clothing, jewelry and personal items up to $900 total(**); household items, furniture, utensils, TVs and radios up to $1,450 total; health aids; cash for sold exempt property; books, pictures and musical instruments up to $300 total(**); food and fuel to last 60 days if debtor is householder; domestic animals and poultry with food to last 60 days up to $1,000; lost earnings payments for debtor or someone debtor depended upon needed for support; personal injury recoveries (not including pain and suffering) up to $7,500(**); $400 of any personal property (but can't be used to increase any existing exemption)(**).

23.166   Bank deposits up to $5,000, and cash for sold exempt items.

23.200   Pistol; rifle or shotgun if owned by person over the age of 16.

61.770   Burial plot.

WAGES

23.185   Minimum of 75% of earned but unpaid wages. Judge may approve more for low income debtor.

PENSIONS

23.170   Federal, state or local government employees.
237.201   Public officers and employees.
239.261   School district employees.

PUBLIC BENEFITS

23.160;147.325   Crime victims' compensation.
344.580   Vocational rehabilitation.
401.405   Civil and disaster relief.
411.760   General assistance.
412.115   Aid to blind.
412.610   Aid to disabled.
413.130   Old-age assistance.
414.095   Medical assistance.
418.040   AFDC
655.530   Injured inmates benefits.
656.234   Workers' compensation.
657.855   Unemployment compensation.

TOOLS OF TRADE

23.160   Tools, library, and team with food to last 60 days, up to $750 total.

ALIMONY AND CHILD SUPPORT

23.160   Alimony and child support needed to support.

INSURANCE

732.240   Life insurance proceeds if policy prohibits use to pay creditors.
743.099   Life insurance proceeds or cash value if you are not the insured.
743.102   Group life insurance policy or proceeds.
743.105   Annuity contract benefits up to $250 per month.
743.108   Health or disability insurance proceeds, dividends, interest, loan, cash or surrender value.
748.225   Fraternal benefit society benefits.

PENNSYLVANIA   References are to Pennsylvania Consolidated Statutes Annotated. Example: "Pa.C.S.A. s.42-8123".

HOMESTEAD: None, but some tenancies by the entirety are exempt without limit.

PERSONAL PROPERTY

42-8123 $300 of any property.
42-8124   Clothing, bibles, school books, sewing machines, uniform and accoutrements.
42-8125   Tangible personal property at an international exhibition sponsored by the U.S. government.

WAGES

42-8127   Earned but unpaid wages.

PENSIONS

16-4716   County employees.
24-8533   Public school employees.
42-8124   Self-employment benefits; private retirement benefits if clause prohibits use to pay creditors.
53-764;53-776;
  53-23666   Police officers.
53-881.115   Municipal employees.
53-13445;
53-23572;
  53-39383   City employees.

71-5953   State employees.

PUBLIC BENEFITS

42-8124   Workers' compensation.
43-863   Unemployment compensation.
51-20012   Veterans' benefits.
51-20098   Korean conflict veterans' benefits.
71-180-7.10   Crime victims' compensation.

INSURANCE

42-8124   No-fault automobile insurance proceeds; accident or disability benefits; group life insurance policy or proceeds; fraternal benefit society benefits; life insurance proceeds if policy prohibits use to pay creditors; life insurance annuity contract payments, proceeds or cash value up to $100 per month; life insurance annuity policy, proceeds or cash value if beneficiary is decendent's spouse, child or other dependent.

PERSONAL PROPERTY

7-8-25	Consumer cooperative association holdings up to $50.
9-26-3	Body of a deceased person.
9-26-4	Clothing needed; furniture and family stores of a housekeeper, beds and bedding up to $1,000 total; books up to $300; burial plot; debt owed to you which is secured by a promissory note or bill of exchange.

WAGES

9-26-4	Earned but unpaid wages up to $50; wages of spouse; earned but unpaid wages of a seaman, or if you have received welfare during the year prior to filing for bankruptcy; wages paid to the poor by a charitable organization; earnings of a minor child.
30-7-9	Earned but unpaid wages of a military member on active duty.

PENSIONS

9-26-5	Police officers and firefighters.
28-17-4	Private employees.
36-10-34	State and municipal employees.

PUBLIC BENEFITS

28-33-27	Workers' compensation.
28-41-32	State disability benefits.
28-44-58	Unemployment compensation.
30-7-9	Veterans' disability or survivor benefits.
40-6-14	AFDC; general assistance; aid to blind, aged and disabled.

TOOLS OF TRADE

9-26-4	Working tools up to $50; library of a professional in practice.

INSURANCE

27-4-11	Life insurance proceeds, dividends, interest, loan, cash or surrender value if beneficiary is not the insured.
27-4-12	Life insurance proceeds if policy prohibits use to pay creditors.
27-18-24	Accident or illness proceeds, benefits, dividends, interest, loan, cash or surrender value.
27-25-18	Fraternal benefit society benefits.

HOMESTEAD

15-41-30	Real property, including coop, up to $5,000.(**)

PERSONAL PROPERTY

15-41-30	Motor vehicle up to $1,200; clothing, household goods, furnishings, appliances, books, musical instruments, animals and crops up to $2,500 total; jewelry up to $500; health aids; personal injury and wrongful death recoveries.
15-41-30	IN LIEU OF HOMESTEAD: Burial plot up to $5,000.(**)
15-41-30	IN LIEU OF HOMESTEAD AND BURIAL PLOT: Cash and other liquid assets up to $1,000.

PENSIONS

9-1-1680	Public employees.
9-8-190	Judges and solicitors.
9-9-180	General assembly members.
9-11-270	Police officers.
9-13-230	Firefighters.

PUBLIC BENEFITS

15-41-30	Unemployment compensation; social security; veterans' benefits.
15-41-30; 16-3-1300	Crime victims' compensation.
42-9-360	Workers' compensation.
43-5-190	AFDC; general relief; aid to blind, aged and disabled.

TOOLS OF TRADE

15-41-30	Tools, books and implements of trade up to $750 total.

ALIMONY AND CHILD SUPPORT

15-41-30	Alimony and child support.

INSURANCE

15-41-30	Unmatured life insurance contract (but a credit insurance policy is not exempt); disability or illness benefits; life insurance proceeds from a policy for a person you depended upon which is needed for support; life insurance dividends, interest, loan, cash or surrender value from a policy for a person you depended upon up to $4,000.
38-37-870	Fraternal benefit society benefits.
38-63-40	Life insurance proceeds for a spouse or child up to $25,000.
38-63-50	Life insurance proceeds if policy prohibits use to pay creditors.

SOUTH DAKOTA

References are to South Dakota Codified Laws. Example: "S.D.C.L. s.43-31-1". Ignore volume numbers; look for "title" numbers.

HOMESTEAD

43-31-1; 43-31-2;
43-32-4 — Real property, including mobile home if registered in the State at least 6 months prior to filing bankruptcy, of unlimited value; but cannot exceed 1 acre in a town or 160 acres elsewhere. Sale proceeds are exempt for 1 year after sale up to $30,000 (of unlimited value if you are an unmarried widow or widower, or are over 70). Spouse or child of a deceased owner may also claim exemption. Can't include gold or silver mine, mill or smelter.

PERSONAL PROPERTY

43-45-2 — All debtors may claim clothing; food and fuel to last 1 year; bible; books up to $200; pictures; church pew; burial plot.

43-45-4 — Non-head of family may also claim $2,000 of any personal property.

43-45-5 — Head of family may claim either $4,000 of any personal property, OR furniture and bedding up to $200; books and musical instruments up to $200; tools and library of professional up to $300; tools of a mechanic and stock in trade up to $200; farm machinery, utensils, wagon, sleigh, 2 plows, harrow, and tackle for teams up to $1,250 total; 2 yoke of oxen or a span of horses or mules; 2 cows, 5 swine, 25 sheep with lambs under 6 months, wool, yarn or cloth of sheep, and food for all to last 1 year.

WAGES

15-20-12 — Earned wages owing 60 days prior to filing for bankruptcy, needed for support.

24-8-10 — Wages of prisoners in work programs.

PENSIONS

3-12-115 — Public employees.

9-16-47 — City employees.

PUBLIC BENEFITS

28-7-16 — AFDC.

61-6-28 — Unemployment compensation.

62-4-42 — Workers' compensation.

TOOLS OF TRADE   See Personal Property.

INSURANCE

43-45-6 — Life insurance proceeds if beneficiary is surviving spouse or child up to $10,000.

58-12-4 — Health benefits up to $20,000; endowment or life insurance policy, proceeds or cash value up to $20,000(*).

58-12-8 — Annuity contract proceds up to $250 per month.

58-15-70 — Life insurance proceeds if policy prohibits use to pay creditors.

58-37-68 — Fraternal benefit society benefits.

TENNESSEE

References are to Tennessee Code Annotated. Example: "T.C.A. s.26-2-301". Ignore volume numbers; look for "section" numbers.

HOMESTEAD

26-2-301 — $5,000; $7,500 for joint owners. Some tenancies by the entirety are exempt without limit. Spouse or child of deceased owner may claim. May also claim a life estate or a 2 to 15 year lease.

PERSONAL PROPERTY

26-2-103 — Clothing and storage containers; schools books, pictures, portraits, and bible.

26-2-111 — Health aids; lost earnings payments for yourself or a person you depended upon; personal injury recoveries, not including pain and suffering, up to $7,500; wrongful death recoveries up to $10,000 (LIMIT: total of personal injury claims, wrongful death claims and crime victims' compensation cannot exceed $15,000).

26-2-305;
46-2-102 — Burial plot up to 1 acre.

WAGES

26-2-106;
26-2-107 — Minimum of 75% or earned but unpaid wages, plus $2.50 per week per child. Judge may apporve more for low income debtor.

PENSIONS

8-36-111 — Public employees.

26-2-104 — State and local government employees.

45-9-909 — Teachers.

PUBLIC BENEFITS

26-2-111 — Unemployment compensation; veterans' benefits; social security; local public assistance.

26-2-111;
29-13-111 — Crime victims' compensation up to $5,000, but see LIMIT under Personal Property above.

71-2-216 — Old-age assistance.

71-3-121 — AFDC.

71-4-117 — Aid to blind.

71-4-1112 — Aid to disabled.

TOOLS OF TRADE

26-2-111 — Tools, books and implements of trade up to $750.

ALIMONY AND CHILD SUPPORT

26-2-111 — Alimony only which is owed for at least 30 days prior to filing for bankruptcy.

INSURANCE

26-2-110 — Disability, accident or health benefits, for a resident and citizen of Tennessee.

26-2-111 — Disability or illness benefits.

26-2-304 — Homeowners' insurance proceeds up to $5,000.

56-7-201 — Life insurance proceeds or cash value if beneficiary is the debtor's spouse, child or other dependent.

56-25-208 — Fraternal benefit society benefits.

TEXAS   References of numbers only are to Texas Revised Civil Statutes Annotated. Example: "T.R.C.S.A. s.6228f". Other references are to other subject volumes in the Codes, such as "T.C.A. Property 41.001". Ignore volume numbers.

SPECIAL LIMIT: Total of personal property (except burial plot), wages, tools of trade, and cash value of insurance cannot exceed $15,000 total ($30,000 for head of family).

HOMESTEAD
Prop. 41.001;
  Prop. 41.002   Unlimited amount, but cannot exceed 1 acre in a city, town or village, or 100 acres (200 acres for family) elsewhere. Sale proceeds are exempt for 6 months after sale. You need not occupy at time of filing bankruptcy as long as you don't acquire another home.

PERSONAL PROPERTY
Prop. 41.001   Burial plots.
Prop. 42.001;
42.002   Clothing, including jewelry; pets; furnishings; heirlooms; food; athletic and sporting equipment; 2 firearms; 1 breeding-age bull, 5 cows with calves, 20 hogs, 20 goats, 20 sheep, 50 chickens, 30 geese, 30 ducks, 30 turkeys, 30 guineas, and forage for all; AND EITHER (a)cars and light trucks not for work, OR (b)any 2 of the following: car, camper, truck, cab or trailer; motorcycle or bicycle; horse, colt, mule or donkey with gear; or wagon, cart, dray and harness; up to $15,000 total ($30,000 for head of family). SEE SPECIAL LIMIT ABOVE.

WAGES
Prop. 42.002   Earned but unpaid wages. SEE SPECIAL LIMIT ABOVE.

PENSIONS
110B-21.005   State employees.

110B-31.005   Teachers.
110B-41.004   Judges.
110B-51.006   County and district employees.
6228f   Law enforcement officers' survivors.
6243d-1;6243j;
  6243g-1   Police officers.
6243e;6243e.1;
  6243e.2   Firefighters.
6243g;
110B-61.006   Municipal employees.
Prop. 42.0021   Church benefits; retirement benefits to extent tax-deferred, including IRAs, Keoghs and simplified employee plans.

PUBLIC BENEFITS
5221b-13   Unemployment compensation.
8306-3   Workers' compensation.
8309-1   Crime victims' compensation.
Hum.Res. 31.040   AFDC.
Hum.Res. 32.036   Medical assistance.

TOOLS OF TRADE
Prop. 42.002   Tools, books, and equipment, including boat; implements of farming or ranching neede for work. SEE SPECIAL LIMITATION ABOVE.

INSURANCE
Insur. 3.50-2   Texas employee uniform group insurance.
Insur. 3.50-3   Texas state college or university employee benefits.
Insur. 3.50-4   Retired public school employees group insurance.
Insur. 10.28   Fraternal benefit society benefits.
Insur. 21.22   Life, health, accident or annuity benefits; life insurance proceeds if policy prohibits use to pay creditors.
Prop. 42.002   Life insurance cash value if policy owned at least 2 years. SEE SPECIAL LIMIT ABOVE.

UTAH   References are to Utah Code. Example: "U.C. s.78-23-3". Ignore volume numbers; look for "title" numbers.

HOMESTEAD
78-23-3   Real property, mobile home or water rights up to $8,000, plus $2,000 for spouse and $500 for each other dependent. Homestead declaration must be filed before selling home.

PERSONAL PROPERTY
78-23-5   Clothing, except furs and jewelry; refrigerator, freezer, stove, washer, dryer and sewing machine; health aids needed; food to last 3 months; beds and bedding; carpets; artwork done by, or depicting, a family member; burial plot; personal injury recoveries for yourself or a person you depend upon; wrongful death recoveries for a person you depended upon.
78-23-8   Furnishings and appliances up to $500; books, musical instruments and animals up to $500 total; heirloom or sentimental item up to $500.
78-23-9   Proceeds for damaged personal property.

WAGES
70C-7-103   Minimum of 75% of earned but unpaid wages. Judge may approve more for low income debtor.

PUBLIC BENEFITS
35-1-80   Workers' compensation.
35-2-35   Occupational disease disability benefits.
35-4-18   Unemployment compensation.
55-15-32   AFDC; general assistance.
78-23-5   Veterans' benefits.

TOOLS OF TRADE
39-1-47   Military property of a national guard member.
78-23-8   Motor vehicle up to $1,500; tools, books and implements of trade up to $1,500.

ALIMONY AND CHILD SUPPORT
78-23-5   Child support.
78-23-6   Alimony needed for support.

INSURANCE
31A-9-603   Fraternal benefit society benefits.
78-23-5   Disability, illness, medical or hospital benefits.
78-23-6   Life insurance proceeds if beneficiary is insured's spouse or other dependent, needed for support.
78-23-7   Life insurance policy cash surrender value up to $1,500.

VERMONT

References are to Vermont Statutes Annotated. Example: "V.S.A. s.27-101".

HOMESTEAD

27-101 $30,000. Some tenancies by the entirety are exempt without limit. May include outbuildings, rents, issues and profits. Spouse of a deceased owner may claim.

PERSONAL PROPERTY

12-2740   Motor vehicles up to $2,500; clothing, goods, furnishings, appliances, books, musical instruments, animals and crops up to $2,500 total; refrigerator, stove, freezer, water heater, heating unit and sewing machines; health aids; bank deposits up to $700; wedding ring; jewelry up to $500; 500 gallons of oil, 5 tons of coal or 10 cords of firewood; 500 gallons of bottled gas; lost future earnings for yourself or a person you depended upon; personal injury and wrongful death recoveries for a person you depended upon; 1 cow, 10 sheep, 10 chickens, 3 swarms of bees, and feed to last 1 winter; 1 yoke of oxen or steers, 2 horses, 2 harnesses, 2 halters, 2 chains, 1 plow and 1 ox yoke; growing crops up to $5,000.

12-2740 $400 of any property; plus $7,000, less any amount claimed for clothing, goods, furnishings, appliances, books, musical instruments, animals, crops, motor vehicle, jewelry, tools of trade and growing crops, of any property.

WAGES

12-3170   Minimum of 75% of earned but unpaid wages (judge may approve more for low income debtor); all wages if you received welfare during the 2 months prior to filing for bankruptcy.

PENSIONS

3-476   State employees.

12-2740   Self-directed accounts, including IRAs and Keoghs, up to $10,000; other pensions.

16-1946   Teachers.

24-5066   Municipal employees.

PUBLIC BENEFITS

12-2740   Veterans' benefits, social security and crime victims' compensation needed for support.

21-681   Workers' compensation.

21-1376   Unemployment compensation.

33-2575   AFDC; general assistance; aid to blind, aged and disabled.

TOOLS OF TRADE

12-2740   Tools and books of trade up to $5,000.

ALIMONY AND CHILD SUPPORT

12-2740   Alimony and child support needed for support.

INSURANCE

8-3705   Life insurance proceeds if policy prohibits use to pay creditors.

8-3706   Life insurance proceeds if insured is not the beneficiary.

8-3708   Group life or health benefits.

8-3709   Annuity contract benefits up to $350 per month.

8-4478   Fraternal benefit society benefits.

12-2740   Unmatured life insurance contract (but not credit insurance policy); disability or illness benefits needed for support; life insurance proceeds for a person you depended upon.

VIRGINIA

References are to Code of Virginia. Example: "C.V. s.34-4". Ignore volume numbers; look for "title" numbers.

HOMESTEAD

34-4; 34-4.1;
34-18 $5,000 ($7,000 for veterans). Some tenancies by the entirety are exempt without limitation. Includes rents and profits. Sale proceeds are exempt up to $5,000. Must file homestead declaration prior to filing for bankruptcy.

PERSONAL PROPERTY

11-28   Burial plot or money paid for a plot up to $500.

34-26   ONLY IF YOU ARE A HOUSEHOLDER YOU MAY CLAIM: Clothing and wardrobes; wedding and engagement rings; beds, bedsteads and bedding; refrigerator, freezer or icebox; oven; stove; washer; dryer up to $150; sewing machine; loom; spinning wheel; 2 basins and 1 table; dining table and 6 chairs; 2 dressers and 2 tables; buffet; cabinet or press; china press; 12 dishes, 12 knives 12 forks, 24 spoons, 6 plates, and 1 pot (if more than 12 in family, may keep 1 more of each of these); cooking utensils; 6 wood or earthenware; kitchen safe; chifforobes; books; pictures; pets; deck of cards; carpets, rugs, linoleum or other floor coverings; 1 axe and 2 hoes; 1 cow and calf; 1 horse; 3 hogs; fowl up to $25; forage and hay; 200 lbs of bacon or pork; 50 bushels of corn or 25 bushels of rye/buckwheat; 20 bushels of potatoes; 5 bushels of wheat or 1 barrel of flour; canned and frozen food; other food up to $50.; 3 appendages.

34-13   IN LIEU OF HOMESTEAD: $5,000 of any personal property.

WAGES

34-29   Minimum of 75% of earned but unpaid wages or pension payments. Judge may approve more for low income debtor.

PENSIONS

51-111.15   State employees.

51-127.7   County employees.

51-180   Judges.

PUBLIC BENEFITS

19.2-368.12   Crime victims' compensation, unless seeking to discharge debt for treatment of crime-related injury.

60.2-600   Unemployment compensation.

63.1-88   AFDC; general relief; aid to blind, aged and disabled.

65.1-82   Workers' compensation.

TOOLS OF TRADE

IF YOU ARE A HOUSEHOLDER YOU MAY CLAIM:

34-26   Tools and utensils of a mechanic; boat and tackle of an oysterman or fisherman up to $1,500.

34-27   For farmer: tractor, wagon, cart, horses, pair of mules with gear up to $3,000; fertilizer, 2 plows, harvest cradle, 2 iron wedges, pitchfork and rake, up to $1,000.

IF NOT A HOUSEHOLDER YOU MAY CLAIM:

44-96   Arms, uniforms and equipment of a military member.

INSURANCE

38.2-3122   Life insurance proceeds, dividends, interest, loan, cash or surrender value if beneficiary is not the insured.

38.2-3123   If you are a householder, life insurance cash values up to $10,000.

38.2-3339   Group life insurance policy or proceeds.

38.2-3549   Accident, sickness or industrial sick benefits.

38.2-3811   Cooperative life insurance benefits.

38.2-4021   Burial society benefits.

38.2-4118   Fraternal benefit society benefits.

51-111.67:8   Group life or accident insurance for government officials.

HOMESTEAD
6.13.010;
6.13.030   Real property or mobile home up to $30,000. If property is unimproved or unoccupied at time of filing bankruptcy, you must file a homestead declaration.

PERSONAL PROPERTY
6.15.010   Motor vehicle up to $1,200; clothing, but furs limited to $750 total; jewelry and ornaments; household goods, furniture, appliances, home and yard equipment up to $1,500 total; food and fuel to last 3 months; books up to $1,000; pictures and keepsakes.; $500 of any other personal property, but not more that $100 of it in cash, bank deposits, stocks, bonds or other securities.

68.20.120   Burial plots if sold by a non-profit cemetary association.

WAGES
6.27.150   Minimum of 75% of earned but unpaid wages. Judge may approve more for low income debtor.

PENSIONS
6.15.020   Federal employees.
41.24.240   Volunteer firefighters.
41.28.200   City employees.
41.40.380   Public employees.

43.43.310   State patrol officers.

PUBLIC BENEFITS
50.40.020   Unemployment compensation.
51.32.040   Industrial insurance (workers' compensation).
74.04.280   General assistance.
74.08.210   Old-age assistance.
74.13.070   AFDC (child welfare).

TOOLS OF TRADE
6.15.010   Tools and materials used in another person's trade up to $3,000; library, office furniture, equipment and supplies of a physician, surgeon, attorney, clergyman or other professional up to $3,000; farm trucks, tools, equipment, supplies, stock and seed of a farmer up to $3,000.

INSURANCE
6.15.030   Fire insurance proceeds for destroyed exempt property.
46.18.400   Disability benefits, proceeds, dividends, interest, loan, cash or surrender value.
46.18.410   Life insurance proceeds, dividends, interest, loan, cash or surrender value if the insured is not the beneficiary,
46.18.420   Group life insurance policy or proceeds.
46.18.430   Annuity contract proceeds up to $250 per month.
48.36A.180   Fraternal benefit society benefits.

HOMESTEAD
38-10-4   Real or personal property used as a residence up to $7,500. Unused portion may be applied to any other property.

PERSONAL PROPERTY
38-10-4   Motor vehicle up to $1,200; clothing, household goods, furnishings, appliances, books, musical instruments, animals and crops up to $200 per item, and $1,000 total; jewelry up to $500; health aids; lost earnings payments needed for support; personal injury recoveries, not including pain and suffering, up to $7,500; wrongful death recoveries for a person you depended upon needed for support.

38-10-4 $7,900, less amount of homestead claimed, of any property.

38-10-4   IN LIEU OF HOMESTEAD: Burial plot up to $7,500.

WAGES
38-5A-3   80% of earned but unpaid wages. Judge may approve more for low income debtor.

PENSIONS
5-10-46   Public employees.
18-7A-30   Teachers.

PUBLIC BENEFITS
9-5-1   AFDC; general assistance; aid to blind, aged and disabled.
14-2A-24;
38-10-4   Crime victims' compensation.
23-4-18   Workers' compensation.
38-10-4   Unemployment compensation; veterans' benefits; social security.

TOOLS OF TRADE
38-4-10   Tools, books and implements of trade up to $750.

ALIMONY AND CHILD SUPPORT
38-10-4   Alimony and child support needed for support.

INSURANCE
33-6-27   Life insurance proceeds unless you are policy owner and beneficiary.
33-6-28   Group life insurance policy and proceeds.
33-23-21   Fraternal benefit society benefits.
38-10-4   Unmatured life insurance contract; health or disability benefits; life insurance dividends, interest, loan, cash or surrender value for person you depended upon up to $4,000.
48-3-23   Life Insurance proceeds or cash value if the beneficiary is a married woman.

WISCONSIN   References are to Wisconsin Statutes Annotated. Example: "W.S.A. s.815.20".

HOMESTEAD

815.20	$40,000. Sale proceed exempt for 2 years after sale provided you intend to acquire another home. Must occupy or intend to occupy at time of filing for bankruptcy.

PERSONAL PROPERTY

815.18	Automobile up to $1,000; clothing; beds, bedsteads and bedding; furniture and cooking utensils up to $200 total; stoves; sewing machines; jewelry and articles of adornment up to $400; food and fuel to last 1 year; books; pictures; firearms up to $50; TV and radio; books, plates and swords given to you by the legislature; burial plot; church pew or seat; U.S. savings bonds up to $200; patents; 10 swine, 10 sheep with wool; 8 cows, 2 horses or mules, 50 chickens, 1 harness, and feed for livestock; sleigh and accessories.
815.18	IN LIEU OF HOMESTEAD: Bank deposits up to $1,000.

WAGES

815.18	Earned but unpaid wages for 30 days; if no dependents, no less than $75 and no more than $100; if you have dependents, $120 plus $20 per dependent, but not to exceed 75% of wages.

PENSIONS

40.08	Public employees.
66.81	Certain municipal employees.
815.18	Police officers, firefighters, military pensions, and private retirement benefits (including plans for self-employed persons).

PUBLIC BENEFITS

45.35	Veterans' benefits.
49.41	AFDC; other social service payments.
102.27	Workers' compensation.
108.13	Unemployment compensation.

TOOLS OF TRADE

815.18	Tools, implements and stock in trade of a mechanic, merchant, trader or miner up to $200; books, maps, plats, and papers for land abstracts; arms, uniforms and equipment of national guard member; printing materials of a printer or publisher up to $1,500 (but only $400 for wages due to workers); tractor up to $1,500, wagon, cart or dray, springtooth harrow, disc harrow, plow, mower, seeder, corn binder and planter, drag, hay loader, farming utensils, small tools and implements up to $300, or the modern equivalent for any of these.

INSURANCE

614.96	Fraternal benefit society benefits.
632.42	Life insurance proceeds if policy prohibits use to pay creditors.
766.09	Life insurance policy or proceeds if beneficiary is a married woman up to $5,000.
815.18	Health, accident or disability benefits up to $150 per month; federal disability benefits; fire insurance proceeds for destroyed exempt property; life insurance proceeds, dividends, interest, loan, cash or surrender value if the insured is not the beneficiary.

WYOMING   References are to Wyoming Statutes Annotated. Example: "W.S.A. s.1-20-101". Ignore volume numbers; look for "title" numbers..

HOMESTEAD

1-20-101; 1-20-104	Real property up to $10,000; house trailer up to $6,000. Some tenancies by the entirety are exempt without limit. Spouse or child of deceased owner may claim; Must occupy at time of filing for bankruptcy. (**)

PERSONAL PROPERTY

1-20-105	Clothing and wedding rings up to $1,000 total.
1-20-106	Household articles, furniture, bedding and food up to $2,000 per person in the home; school books, pictures and bible.
1-20-106; 35-8-104	Burial plot.
26-32-102	Pre-paid funeral contracts.

WAGES

1-15-511	Minimum of 75% of earned but unpaid wages. Judge may approved more for low income debtor.
19-2-501	Earnings of national guard members.

PENSIONS

9-3-426	Public employees.
9-3-620	Highway officers, criminal investigators, and game and fish wardens.
15-5-209	Payments being received by police officers and firefighters.

PUBLIC BENEFITS

1-40-113	Crime victims' compensation.
27-3-319	Unemployment compensation.
27-14-702	Workers' compensation.
42-2-113	AFDC; general assistance.

TOOLS OF TRADE

1-20-106	Motor vehicle, tools, implements, team and stock in trade to $2,000; library and implements of a professional up to $2,000.\

INSURANCE

26-15-129	Life insurance proceeds if insured is not the beneficiary.
26-15-130	Disability benefits if policy prohibits use to pay creditors.
26-15-131	Group life or disability policy or proceeds.
26-15-132	Annuity contract proceeds up to $350 per month.
26-15-133	Life insurance proceeds if policy prohibits use to pay creditors.
26-29-116	Fraternal benefit society benefits.

INDEX

Self Help Law Books

Available from: Sphinx Publishing, P. O. Box 2005, Clearwater, Florida 34617

National Titles

How to File Your Own Bankruptcy (or How to Avoid it) With Forms $19.95 ☐
Explains how bankruptcy works and how to file bankruptcy with or without an attorney.

How to Register a United States Trademark, 2nd Ed. With Forms $14.95 ☐
Explains types of trademarks and step-by-step procedures for registration.

How to Register a United States Copyright, 2nd Ed. With Forms $14.95 ☐
Explains what can and cannot be copyrighted and step-by-step procedures for registration.

Social Security Benefits Handbook $9.95 ☐
Explains eligibility, applications, Medicare, Disability, Computations, Reductions, Limits, and more.

How to Get a Visa to the U.S.A. $14.95 ☐
Explains types of permanent and temporary visas, eligibility, application process, and more.

How to Draft Real Estate Contracts, 2nd Ed. With Forms $11.95 ☐
Explains each clause used in real estate contracts and includes 5 different forms to save you money.

How to Draft Real Estate Leases, 2nd Ed. With Forms $11.95 ☐
Explains each clause used in leases and includes five leases (residential, commercial and mini-storage).

Florida Titles

How to Start a Business in Florida, 2nd Ed. With Forms $14.95 ☐
Explains Florida laws about fictitious names, licenses, trademarks, partnerships, unemployment compensation, sales tax, regulatory laws, federal taxes, and more.

How to Form a Simple Corporation in Florida, With Forms $14.95 ☐
Explains advantages, disadvantages, types of corporations, start-up procedures, stock laws, etc.

How to File for Divorce in Florida, With Forms $19.95 ☐
Explains Florida laws regarding divorce, property settlements and child custody and support, Includes forms for simplified and uncontested divorces and explains the procedures in simple language.

Landlords' Rights and Duties in Florida 2d Ed., With Forms & Caselaw $14.95 ☐
Explains laws about evictions, security deposits, discrimination, abandoned property, housing codes, bad checks, residential and nonresidential tenancies, self-storage and mobile home parks.

Land Trusts in Florida, 2nd Ed. With Forms & Caselaw $19.95 ☐
Explains how trusts can avoid probate, keep assets secret, avoid liability and litigation, and more.

How to Win in Small Claims Court in Florida, With Forms $14.95 ☐
Explains how to file, settle, argue, defend your case and includes forms for claims, garnishment, etc.

How to Form a Nonprofit Corporation in Florida, With Forms $14.95 ☐
Explains types of nonprofit corps., start-up procedures, charitable solicitation, tax exemptions, etc.

How to Make a Florida Will, With Forms $9.95 ☐
Explains joint tenancy, homestead, spouses' rights, guardians, personal representatives, living wills, I/T/F bank accounts, and more, and includes 14 forms.

How to Raise (or Lower) Your Child Support in Florida, With Forms $14.95 ☐
Explains how to petition the court to modify child support payments, with all forms.

How to Change Your Name in Florida, With Forms $9.95 ☐
Explains Florida laws regarding names and includes forms for changing name with or without court action.

Now available! Legal forms on computer diskettes and books from other publishers. Write for info.

To order use this form or call 1-800-226-5291 for credit card orders. (Sorry, no C.O.D.)

Name _____

Address _____

City, State _____ Zip _____

Subtotal:	_____
Fla. orders add tax (6% or 7%)	_____
Shipping:	$1.50
Total enclosed:	_____

90B